LOVE
SPELLS

Other titles by James Lynn Page:
Applied Visualisation — A Mind–Body Programme

LOVE
SPELLS

James Lynn Page

quantum

LONDON•NEW YORK•TORONTO•SYDNEY

quantum

An imprint of W. Foulsham & Co. Ltd.,
Yeovil Road, Slough, Berkshire SL1 4JH

ISBN 0-572-01621-2

Copyright © 1992 James Lynn Page

Printed in Great Britain by Cox & Wyman Ltd,
Reading, Berkshire

CONTENTS

Love Spells — An Introduction   **7**

1. An Eternal Enigma   **14**
    The eternal search for love; courtly love and the
    Romantics; masculine/feminine opposites.

2. Tao and Tantra   **35**
    The Tao, yin–yang and the nature of human attraction;
    Tantra, the interplay of female and male energies.

3. The Astrology of Love   **45**
    Relationships and the four elements.

4. The Fate Of Relationships   **69**
    Relationships as a mirror of the unconscious; the
    relationship between outer and inner being; soul
    mates.

5. Love Objects — A Warning   **85**
    Differentiating between fantasy and reality; projection
    in relationships.

6. Be Your Own Prophet   **104**
    Relating to the future; creating reality; the prophet
    Merlin as a symbol of transformation.

Love Spells – Practice makes Perfect   **117**

7.   When I Dream — Visualising A Lover   **119**
      Love spells and the use of visualisation techniques.

8.   A Temple To Hekate   **133**
      The goddess of magick; crystal and candle visions;
      bringing ideals into reality; affirmations for authority,
      friendship and love.

Selected Bibliography   **155**

Index   **157**

LOVE SPELLS
AN INTRODUCTION

'Love Spells? It sounds like a book on that witchcraft stuff.'

'What do you mean'? I knowingly enquired.

'You know, devil worship.'

'But it's not about that,' did I protest.

'Well, what's it about then?' he asked.

'Modern relationships, the mystery of attraction, powers of thought, the occult.'

'The occult?' came the trembling reply, as if I had suddenly sprouted Pan's horns. The expression changed and he re-asserted himself, 'What have I just been saying, *devil worship*.'

Sometimes I wish I had never broached the subject at all, for as soon as these archaic, even exotic sounding names are mentioned – occult, divination, sorcery, necromancy, wicca – ears prick up and I find myself in the position of having to justify the merits of esoteric practices and studies falling under the general umbrella of the occult. To a small extent, this is what *Love Spells* is about; almost an apology for using paganish words in a modern technological age.

However, as an Aquarian Age grimoire for the lost and lonely, the major theme underpinning this book is timeless. It serves fundamentally as a practical work-book, commencing with a general philosophy on the human experience of love and concluding with magickal techniques enabling the participant to exercise his or her own mental powers. The result is the successful conclusion of a 'Love Spell'. Perhaps this sounds like an exhortation to take on the mantle of the sorcerer's apprentice, but I am no sorcerer and perhaps you are no acolyte of the Golden Dawn. But perhaps you *are* one of the individuals who inhabit this planet with a need to form an emotional relationship, to experience love and to find a partner. If that is the case, then this book is for you.

Anyone may put the laws of attraction to use via the forces within them, when the correct conditions are satisfied. If it is that longed for partner that occupies your thoughts, if you are waiting for the 'right one to come along', then it is time to commence the inner journey and set to work on drawing that elusive partner into your life. The technique I have chosen for affecting such an apparently miraculous feat is mental imagery. It may seem like nothing short of divine power to be able to attract your dream lover into your personal universe and apparently have an instant relationship. But this is to be ignorant of the underlying principles (and these principles are quite 'real') upon which magick is based. That the forces operating in the mental world are invisible (and thus non-existent for many) often tempts us to forget psychic realities, but as a learned colleague of mine once pointed out, 'once experienced, never forgotten'. I hope that the psychological and magickal tenets among the following chapters will inspire you to take the first step towards realising this basic aim.

The first half of the book reflects upon the eternal search for what has proved so elusive through the ages, perhaps because it is something that cannot really be found 'out there'. Love, and its attendant mysteries is intimately personal and has no independent existence of its own. One cannot 'seek' it in a market-place of human affairs in the same way one may venture out to purchase a leather jacket. One may only establish contact with it through relationship to the rest of life – an experience which amounts to a reflection of one's inner self. Hence, we cannot arrive at any one absolute definition of 'love'. Doing so would only limit whatever it may represent. The world is simply too large a place to begin attaching labels to a timeless, archetypal experience. It is much the same case with analyses of human beings: the world is populated by a staggering number of different personality 'types' who carry with them their polar 'opposite' – from the hardened sceptic to the gullible and credulous; the puritanical to the self-obsessed; the neurotic and bloody-minded to the dry and taciturn; the spiritually aware, non-smoking vegetarian to the more physical type whose raison d'être encompasses nothing more divine than beer, sex, chips and gravy. Yet not one of these 'types' may truly lend themselves to a neatly curtailed objective definition.

Labels do not hold good whenever we attempt to understand human beings. In fact we understand them less as a result. To imprint the tag of 'bore', 'puritan', 'pervert', or whatever upon others has the unfortunate side effect (for the one criticising) of wrapping the object of derision in a kind of invisible strait-jacket from which they are not to be released. In casting such judgements we do not permit our foe any other qualities than the ones with which they have been branded.

Most humans are sensitive enough to respond to this kind of snare. Thus, wherever the twain shall meet again, the one labelled reacts appropriately to his critic with the traits he is condemned with, almost as if unconsciously compelled to display these qualities. This creates a self-perpetuating cycle, for the critic satisfies himself every time that his prey really is 'stupid', 'arrogant', 'weird' or 'backward', remaining unaware that these are the very qualities he happens to extract every time he comes into contact with the other. He remains unaware that the other is simply giving him what he wants. If one were to break this spiral of ignorance by looking a little closer, it would become obvious that human beings do not operate according to fixed labels. They defy all our attempts to pin down their 'personalities', which in itself is just an outer shell. When we learn of someone's actions involving others that contradict our prejudices about them, we may surprise ourselves because we 'never knew they were like that'. Towards us they probably never have been.

This hopefully illustrates just one of the common misunderstandings we create in relating to others. The passing of judgement, the emotional bias and the overfed ego, all contribute to avoiding having to discover oneself and understand others. This is one particular attitude that engenders eventual loneliness. We live in an utterly subjective world to begin with, a world which asserts itself only in relation to 'me'. And if I wish to condemn the world as an unfriendly place, then my beliefs must forever be confirmed as life replays my silent, inner thoughts back to me. Whatever it is ye shall seek, so shall ye find.

So to the contents themselves: Part One is a travelogue through the various philosophies and psychologies of East and West. It affords a glimpse of the way in which human beings have developed their ability to relate to each other. From such schools of thought as classical literature, the 'Romantics', Jungian therapy, Taoism and Astrology, is delivered the message that one lives not in an objective world, but one of appearances that is coloured vividly with one's inner viewpoint. It is often difficult to discern precisely how much (if any at all) objectivity lies 'out there'. However illuminating these subjects be in themselves, one ought to be able to experience their truths directly, thus the reader is taken into the infinite space of his or her own, personal psyche.

Following the journey through the world of personal relationships comes the point of the text which reflects upon the ultimate cause of our trials and tribulations in the area of human relating: ourselves. This means the very thoughts and feelings we entertain about life, and as a colleague of mine once remarked: 'you are your own universe' (though I refused to have it as the title of this book, despite his pleadings). Whenever speaking of mental 'influence', one must turn either to the philosophies of the East, Western psychology, the parapsychological investigations of J.B.

Rhine, or the lamentably unrespectable practices of the occult. What one deals with via the occult is that powerful agency concealed from the eyes of man which is nothing other, or more sinister than, the influence of mind. This force is in itself neither good nor bad (indifferent, certainly) because the mind is a self-asserting entity with its own capacity for making its presence felt in the lives of human beings. And observe its workings we must if we are to entertain a healthy, fulfilling existence.

The mind has a capacity to act spontaneously and draw us unwittingly into situations we often would prefer to avoid. We have been shown over and over again that thought can be utilised to perform apparent miracles upon the central nervous system of the human body – a discovery which gave rise to the proliferation of books and tapes containing techniques on how to 'stop smoking', 'gain/lose weight', etc. These psychosomatic effects though are side effects of what might be achieved through mind-matter interaction. The second half of *Love Spells* deals with the powers of mind, whereby the earnest individual can attempt to attract helpful situations into his or her life from the outside, as it were.

You may begin straight away the mental preparations for your 'Love Spell', by picturing to yourself the ideal image of the partner who will eventually manifest – as if by magic – in your life. Persist in 'seeing' this mystery person in your mind's eye, enjoying the imaginative scenes created in the limitless realms of your mind. *Believe* that such romantic fancies can actually come true, having a wholehearted faith that the powers of the psyche can perform such a transformation. There is then little that can stand in your way. And why? Because the universe is *mental* in nature. Whatever it is we choose to think, feel or believe, eventually finds its way into our life as a concrete event. The only real limitations – as we have heard many times over – are those which we create for ourselves. Perhaps the time is ripe to start encouraging a simple faith in ourselves, a faith empowered, illogical though it may seem, to bring our inner dream into outer reality.

I will show more precisely, with the technique of visualisation, how you may draw into your personal world the ideal relationship you have longed for. *That* is what *Love Spells* is all about. Devil worship, indeed. God forbid.

Yield To Love

An inscription above the magnificent stone fireplace at Cardiff Castle reads 'Love conquers all: let us yield to love,' serving both as a statement and a plea to allow a force far mightier than man to enter his soul and, presumably, open the door to the truth. From the passage in Genesis that asserts that God created both man and woman, where one is led to suspect that some binding force helps them to enjoy each other's company, to the successful relationships engendered in the twentieth century, we are most certainly no nearer to unravelling the mystery that we call 'love'. It has been mythologised as an impersonal force in classical Greece as Eros, as the generative power that precipitated the marriage of heaven and earth; personified in Venus and her offspring, elevated to spiritual levels and defined in a myriad of human modes of expression. It has been called transforming, numinous, necessary, creative, an inspiration, enchanting, a force from above, a kind of warfare and a disease.

But however we choose to label 'it', the fact remains that our relationships are generally in an unhealthy state. A peek at the agony columns in the gossip press is enough to make one sufficiently aware of this. Whether this sorry state of affairs (no pun intended) is due to our not knowing how to love properly, a lack of self-understanding, not enough sympathy with the Women's Lib movement or the general lack of moral fibre in today's society, no-one is really in a position to say. Certainly at the root of this problem lies man's and woman's handling of their relationships.

The complications engendered by love, romance, togetherness, union – call it what you will – are not assuaged by various self-appointed 'authorities' on the prickly matters of male-female partnership (and with this remark, I do not refer to counsellors and therapists) whose pearls of wisdom usually confuse and blur the issues even more. This is because they assume that their subjective opinions must necessarily count for everyone else too, even when speaking about love: 'the proper subject for love is one's equal, as the essence of love is to be mutual . . . ' Perhaps the author of this would like to explain just how one goes about finding a 'proper subject', i.e. one's equal, in a world already populated with lonely individuals who would be only too glad of a little human affection from the opposite sex, equal or unequal.

Nor are our confusions about love relationships helped much by the so-called great minds of our time, for when Sigmund Freud blandly called love 'aim-inhibited sex', and Theodore Reik defines it as ' . . . a substitute for the vain urge to reach one's ego ideal', I am left wondering whether or not these men actually expected to be taken seriously. Love may have been the result of a deflected sex drive to Freud, but that was Freud's problem. What I am opposed to, are such airtight definitions of a thoroughly elusive entity such as love. For when we have defined precisely what something *is*, we are also, in effect, saying what it is not, whereupon we tend to forget that no one human being can ever define reality for another. Perhaps we ought to simply heed the injunction at Cardiff Castle, for it is also requesting that we abandon our pre-judgements of others, such inner bias being a reflection of something we cannot deal with in ourselves. If I were to rewrite that inscription it would read: 'Awareness conquers all: let us strive for awareness.' But of course it doesn't have quite the same ring.

CHAPTER 1

AN ETERNAL ENIGMA

'Nobody has measured, even poets, how much a human heart can hold.'
Zelda Fitzgerald

My dictionary offers the definition of the word 'enigma' as a 'puzzling thing or riddle', and describes 'eternal' as 'without beginning or end'. Love, as one of the great archetypal human mysteries, may perhaps be described thus. Consider the endless longings trapped within the unconscious depths of man and woman goading them into the search for love. In particular, consider the self-questioning mortal bearing the scars of rejection and filled with disgust at their own lot, who can only conclude that the need for love is, in the final analysis, a perpetual mystery.

Anyone who has undergone this soul-searching, often crucifying experience, knows intuitively that it stems not simply from a desire for human companionship, candelit dinners, a substitute parent or even physical affection. One is spurred on by some intense, unexplainable longing which resides, with pained hunger, in the very depths of one's soul. It is a yearning so profound that the thing sought proves to be something that the individual feels he or she cannot live without. It is plainly felt that true happiness never really arises without someone to love. Moreover, no amount of diagnoses from the psychoanalyst such as 'mother-complex', 'father-complex' or 'obsessional neurosis', will ever gloss over the fact of personal emptiness, much less 'cure' the patient.

One might even conclude that man's need for a mate is a rather uncomfortable thorn in his side, for were it not so he would not be tormented by the grief of lost love, insatiable sexual desires and the hunger for deep emotional union. (And this, of course, applies not only to the male.) I have encountered often the remark by male and female friends that life would be so much simpler without the hassles that a love relationship constitutes. Some of them have seemingly given up trying in this area of life, preferring the safety of being alone. Yet those who would make the effort to love someone else – despite their quirks and imperfections – will hopefully find it worth the effort and should the relationship fail, learn well what the experience has taught them. Love remains both a blessing and a curse, a fount source of inspiration and the begetter of black despair, yet for some it is a dimly lit road down which they *must* travel, despite the double-edged sword. Says philosopher Bertrand Russell in his autobiography, 'I have sought love, first because it brings ecstasy – ecstasy so great that I would have sacrificed all the rest of life for a few hours of this joy. I have sought it, next because it relieves loneliness – that terrible loneliness in which one's shivering consciousness looks over the rim of the world into the cold, unfathomable life abyss.'

As we can see, the quest for love – at least as far as Russell is concerned – is an inescapable fact of human psychology, a propellant to relieve one from the horrors of loneliness, mind-numbing solitude and the plague of that fearful emptiness from which one peers into the 'cold, unfathomable life abyss'. The author of *Don Quixote*, Miguel Cervantes, likewise views the eternal enigma as an impending, irresistible force emerging from the depths of one's being. We had better understand precisely what it is that gorges upon the soul, moreover, what it asks of us, lest we recoil in terror at such a pernicious being: 'Love, I've heard it said, sometimes flies and sometimes walks, with one it runs and with another it creeps, some it cools and some it burns, some it wounds and others it kills . . . in the morning it makes a siege to a fortress and by evening it conquers it, for there is no force that can resist it. That being so, what is it that frightens you?' Indeed, both bliss and anxiety sit conspicuously beside one another as the distracting muse guides us on the quest for emotional fulfilment.

Possibly the greatest exponents of this uniquely personal journey are the names of historical literature associated with what has come to be known as the Romantic movement, among them writers of such calibre as the Brontës, Goethe, Shelley, Byron, Melville, and Rousseau. The Romantic movement flowered between approximately 1770 and 1848 and delivered work of masterly penetration and sublime depth. Today's psychiatrist, after reading a few lines, might well conclude that here is 'enough material for an entire conference'. Yet the Romantics' greatness lay, and still lies, in encapsulating the dramas of the human heart into moving and meaningful prose:

> Astarte! my beloved! speak to me
> I have so much endured – so much to endure
> Thou lovedst me too much, as I loved thee
> We were not made to torture thus each other

wrote Byron in his 1817 work *Manfred*, in which the title character laments the death of his lover in a vain attempt to summon her ghostly spirit. Through such powerful verbal tapestries we are exposed to the immortal longings of the soul, to love's fatally consuming aspect. For example, the feelings of vengeful spite fostered by unrequited love are portrayed in Charles Baudelaire's *Flowers of Evil*:

> You, who like a dagger plunged
> Into my heart with deadly thrills
> You, who stronger than a crowd
> Of demons, mad, and dressed to kill.

Of course, no-one today would be found uttering such verbiage, except perhaps in the theatre, yet the passions of

16

the heart remain stubborn and uncompromising. Such poetical language, particularly that of the Romantics, resonates deeply within. It finds a sympathetic ear in the heart. Anyone suffering the anguish of lost love will hear only too well the whispers of raw sentiment one finds in the poetry of the Romantic movement.

Perhaps not surprisingly, the Romantics have been criticised for the morose qualities of their work, and it is indeed a recurrent theme – as if melancholy were a virtue to pursue in its own right – a feature of Byron, especially. However, the essential feature shared by the Romantics is the Great Vision, noble and dramatic, a vision inspired by the hungry soul's longing for the beautiful ideal to manifest. Such a muse for the Romantic may be found in the lakeside scene, the pastoral meadow in summer (à la Constable), the remote Gothic castle, and in particular, the subject of love and its inspirational properties. The passions amplified by such writers, in stark contrast to the (then) prevailing Age of Reason, is brilliantly summarised by David Daiches in his introduction to the later editions of Emily Brontë's *Wuthering Heights*: '[Such emotions are] the most powerful, most irresistible and the most tenacious of forces that reside in the depths of human nature [and] have no relation with the artificial world of civilization and gentility.'

That 'artificial world', as far as matters of the heart are concerned, spread into full bloom several hundred years before the Romantic movement, with the advent of the period of courtly love. Mediaeval troubadours would then humbly place themselves in the service of their Fair Lady. Love-sick courtiers might pine incessantly for the heart of their beloved. Perhaps the most widely known example is that of Sir Lancelot and Queen Guinevere from the tales of Chretien De Troyes, which fully portray the nature and mannerisms of 'courting', a tradition firmly ingrained within the collective modern psyche. Courtly love, in the thirteenth century, was a refinement and homogenisation of sensual, earthly desires into something noble, virtuous, and above all, cerebral. To all intents and purposes it remains a sterile passion not permitted to emanate from below the belt. The traces of this may be seen today in the 'conventional' couple who must in social situations avoid the unutterable word. They must present to parents and friends alike what is agreed are the more respectable and clean aspects of a loving relationship.

The traditions of courtly love are born from the individual's need to conform to what society expects, which, in the Middle Ages, was guided by the Church. It was during this period that attempts were made by certain writers to formalise the practice of love. In the *Art of Loving* by Andreas Capellanus, no less than thirty-one 'rules' of love are set down as guidelines for the proper conduct in such matters, and what one may or may not do with one's hands at any particular given moment. Rule twelve, for instance, states that: 'The true lover desires no embraces from any other than the beloved', a rule which turned out to be unworkable in the extreme. Even the noble knight was apt to fall short of his chivalric ideals and allow his attentions to stray elsewhere from the beloved. Like most imperfect humans his passions might be aroused by someone other than his so-called Lady Fair, and he could no longer lay claim to the title of 'true lover'. However, so much for mediaeval relationship counselling.

There is a world of difference between courtly love and the true passions of the Romantics. The former traces boundaries around the nebulous world of the human heart. The individual is then torn between the natural drives of instinct, and the external values enforced from without – be they from the Church, the government, parents, employers or the moral majority. The individual thus becomes alienated from powerful feelings – whether passionate love, hate, thirst for living – if he bows too far to the collective standards we have lamentably inherited from the mediaeval period. These standards have engendered the repression and blind ignorance of man's 'natural' side. The modern nuclear age witnesses the individual, to paint a broad outline, as a society-conscious, well-educated being, attempting to further intellectual/material ends; not as someone attempting to get to grips with complex emotional issues. One who attempts to understand the language of the emotions has on his hands a typical human dilemma, for he needs to give voice to the world of human emotion in a society that does not value it. A sensitive person will thus be afraid to express himself.

Much of the noteworthy efforts of depth psychology are directed towards getting the individual to understand that supposed inner demons may be a result of an unnatural suppression of vital feelings. The Romantics gave voice to those vital feelings, the forces that must be dealt with in oneself. Their power is not diminished by a few visits to the psychiatrist's couch, though of course, it may help one to understand them better. This is a far cry from the gaily stitched sentiments regarding love in traditional courting, for with the poetical legacy left by Goethe, Blake, Shelley and co., we are in the domain of modern psychology and the effects of interpersonal exchange. The difference between courtly love and that experienced by the Romantics is the difference between a fair maiden simpering in crinolines whilst her lord and master is absent, and the terrible, poisonous rage invoked through having been spurned; it is the difference between the petals of a rosebud and the thorns which lie beneath; between what is usually considered as 'nice', pleasant and attractive and what is neither pleasant nor nice but disquieting, unprepossessing and certainly no less attractive. In short, it is the difference between the fickle creations of the intellect and the gut sentiments of the heart. What inspired Romantic poetry and fiction may be encapsulated in one word: passion. Such writing carries with it dramatic overtones and a sense of unfathomable depth. The heart *is* dramatic, and poetry comes directly from the heart. French novelist Albert Camus writes, 'An intense feeling carries with it its own universe, magnificent or wretched as the case may be.'

'De Gustibus Non Disputandum Est'

Or if you prefer, one ought not to quarrel about tastes – an ancient Roman injunction with profound ramifications. It may, and does indeed to some, contradict all reason that one could be attracted to something neither 'pleasant nor nice'. Yet what constitutes something being attractive has little to do with surface pleasantries. In the true sense of the word, 'attractive' is whatever contains drawing-power and magnetism. The logic of the heart is absurd indeed. If anyone would care to disagree with the axiom that one cannot account for personal preferences, then perhaps they would like to explain why natives of the Trobrian Island prefer females in possession of physical features that would normally be regarded as unattractive by any Westerner. According to Lailan Young in *Love Around The World*, there is always someone, somewhere, who will love you no matter what you look like, which presumably accounts for certain male native's fascination for women with black teeth and/or gums, hideous facial features and calves the size of rugby balls.

It is nonetheless typical for us to condemn our neighbour's personal taste as wrong, as if this valuing process was indeed an appropriate subject for rights or wrongs. This moral standpoint in personal affairs falls like a ton of bricks upon the more intimate matters of human relating, particularly that of sexual behaviour. This ancient mystery, owing to its intensely subjective nature, is hopelessly misrepresented by minds who believe that bringing it out into the open (no pun intended) will prove the solution to our inner phobias regarding sex. One can no more rationalise about sexual matters than one can argue that Marilyn Monroe was a great actress. Any such attempts at reaching a final 'objective' conclusion must in the end bow to personal taste – even when speaking of the taboo area of so-called 'sexual aberrations'.

The American Psychiatric Association has, for our everlasting benefit, coined the term 'paraphiliac' to denote the individual whose sexual nature is 'abnormal', and one may rest assured that they have already concluded in advance what is to be considered 'normal'. If by abnormal they are referring to such out-of-bounds areas as voyeurism, trans-vestism, fetishism (thank you, Professor Freud), exhibition-ism, or sex over the telephone, then we are to ascertain that certain drives within the human psyche must be very sick indeed and in need of a hasty cure. Yet these unspeakable practices hold a great fascination for many 'abnormal' indi-viduals for as Roman orator Tacitus points out, 'Things forbidden have a secret charm'. The attraction to these 'things forbidden' is expressive of the private world of the individual.

In having pigeonholed the sexual nature of the individual into an either/or, situation, we commit the age-old error of establishing a boundary, a perimeter fence, around a natur-ally boundless, free-flowing entity, i.e. the psyche. The un-conscious is a-moral, in that the instincts emerging forth from the inner psyche are quite ignorant of the moralistic conceptions of the civilised ego.

Perhaps it is symptomatic of the Aquarian Age's collective, yet slow, gravitation towards openness and freedom that we are witnessing a kind of sexual revolution, where former values are being stood on their head. Partners' roles in a relationship are no longer necessarily based on their gen-ders. Society has not been slow in labelling, and gloating about, for instance, the 'cradle snatcher' phenomenon, whereby one might indeed meet the new step mother at the wedding reception only to discover that she is ten years younger than oneself.

In the same vein, one might read somewhere of pension-age grandfathers tying the knot with girls barely out of teenage; probably the same former little girl who would have sat in his lap whilst he read *Goldilocks* to her. Yet as in the true spirit of the Age of Aquarius, it would be immensely unfair and discriminating to see a preponderance of older men marrying young women, thus do we herald the arrival of the emancipated, middle-aged Career Woman with her consort –

the handsome blond prince in a smart suit who has barely begun to shave. This particular variation of the world of human relating has hitherto been belittled, to use the gutter press appelation, as the 'toy-boy' phenomenon. The worldly and financially solvent woman reverses the age-old master/mistress arrangement. She just might well only be interested in his anatomy. (Sexism inverted, no less.)

Today we are accustomed to the term 'sexist', a practice that has become almost as taboo and sinful as it was to utter the word 'Jehovah' in biblical times. For some women, if a male is considered 'sexist' because of the unspeakable remarks he has made, the shock and outrage thus invoked is often tantamount to that felt at a common criminal getting away (literally) with murder.

To be sexist, we are told, is to denigrate women, tacitly to assert one's superiority over the female. What must surely stand as the all-time hackle raiser for feminists is that sexism equals the treatment of women as sexual objects. Page Three models, quite expectedly, come under the proverbial hammer from fundamentalist women's libbers, who can be a source of amusement to those who find their objections a mite obsessive, fanatical, and even unintelligent. Even the more perceptive figureheads and writers on feminism seem threatened by this fantasy for men staring out invitingly from a cheap newspaper. They feel somehow let down by their own sex for willingly participating in the glamourised projections of the male psyche. Joan Smith, in her book *Mysoginies*, expresses it thus: 'Page three is, by its very nature, the antithesis of the erotic and [reduces] the male sexual response to little more than a visually induced wank.'

Tied in with this reaction to sexism is of course the objection to the Masculine Myth as it has been portrayed in popular culture. For instance in modern consumer ads. (especially during the sixties) for cigarettes, cars and Scotch whisky, we see portrayed the typical 'man's world' and his beloved possessions – the bikini clad 'dolly bird' set against an exotic backdrop of sun, sea and sky, and the gleaming

E-type Jaguar car which he will undoubtedly refer to as 'she' when discussing its merits with his business associates in his private club. The Masculine Myth is also portrayed in the image of the 'typical' male posing masterfully for the camera, accompanied by the ubiquitous glass of whisky and the even more ubiquitous female playmate staring back at him.

Such an image of superlative masculinity reached its apotheosis in the figure of fictional superspy James Bond 007. This is a good example with which to approach the basic feminist arguments that women are used as nothing more than empty vessels for the fantasies of the male. Indistinguishable from this viewpoint is that, portrayed thus, women are on the whole submissive and empty-headed items of decoration. It is usually such an image of femininity which comes across in Ian Fleming's books, where women furnish Bond's world of guns, hotel rooms, casinos, hoodlums and dry Martinis like some decorative vase of plastic flowers – attractive but ultimately disposable. When, in the film version of *Goldfinger*, Jill Masterson is discovered dead and covered entirely in gold paint, or when Aki, Bond's Japanese paramour in *You Only Live Twice*, is accidentally poisoned, the impression is created that women ought not to be mixed up in such a dangerous, rough-and-tough 'Man's world'.

Thus is projected the age-old idea of what are specifically the roles females are supposed to perform, and by and large they fall into only two categories: the purring sex kitten, an object of erotic fantasy; and the housewife/mother, an image of mundane reality. It is these two exaggerated stereotypes of the female – the Marilyn Monroe icon and the dutiful frump – which tend to outrage those of the feminist persuasion. One can understand full well the reaction to womanhood being portrayed as the hideous battleaxe so beloved of TV programmes like Benny Hill and Coronation St., but I believe that the issue of woman-as-sex-object requires much closer inspection. For instance, the sexy, female provocateuse, the object of a hundred-and-one wolf-whistles is a well recognised source of annoyance to many feminists. So too is the woman who boasts of her appearance between the covers of *Playboy* magazine.

What is not so well documented are the opinions and perspectives of the women themselves who pose naked in 'magazines for men', or who attend telephone chat lines to perform imaginary lewd activities with their sexually frustrated male callers – what do *these* ladies think of the women-as-sex-objects issue? I am reminded here of a comment once made by the notorious Cynthia Payne, who said quite plainly and frankly: 'Man wants sex, woman wants money,' an aphorism which, despite its obvious oversimplification, contains more than a grain of truth. If the popularity of blue movies, pornographic magazines and kinky phone lines is any yardstick to measure by, then we are lead to the conclusion that the female participants of these forms of entertainment see them as a rather facile way of making money, and little else. And then there is the 'glamour' model, displayed on countless glossy calendars, who can justify her revealing career by the amount of money she is paid, for as far as she is concerned, she is just a hard-working model.

The money issue does not fully inform us of the glamour girl's perspective on sexism. For example, what about the girl one might espy in a local pub or restaurant at the weekend 'on the town', in her sexy attire, lips red and pouting, eyes beautiful and bedroom-ready? Is she projecting this image because she believes men prefer sex-objects, because that is her only possible chance of attracting a member of the opposite sex, or could it be that she is doing it for her own sake, because she likes to be noticed? The controversy evoked on this issue by women stems not only from the male's so-called degradation of women – it has arisen throughout history often by a secret collusion between males *and* females. Some women actually enjoy dressing in provocative clothes, actually enjoy the wolf-whistles, and don't feel degraded at all in such situations.

Whilst many changes in attitudes towards women have

finally been brought about, and advertisers, book publishers, film producers and media executives are more acutely aware of the present women's movement and all that it stands for, the feminist label, associated with militant, men-hating bra-burners, has unfortunately stuck. It is this particular label which prevents a truer understanding of the philosophy underpinning the women's movement: 'And the irony is that it emerged from a philosophy that set out to destroy the whole notion of female tagging' (Lynda Hurst, *The Toronto Star*,1980).

The problem of female tagging is an old one. The assumption persists that women are nothing more than an employee of the kitchen sink, good for only 'women's things'. Consequently, it is felt by certain feminists that men are basically women haters, and in some cases – when one reads the comments of some 'great minds' – one is tempted to agree with them wholeheartedly. Here is a sample of various 'misogynies', ranging from the impertinent, to the malicious, to the completely moronic:

'Woman is a miserable creature, always inferior to man.' Marquis De Sade (1740-1844)

'When thou goeth to woman, forget not thy whip.' Friedrich Nietzsche (1844-1900)

'Certain women should be struck regularly, like gongs.' Noel Coward (1899-1973)

'Three things have been difficult to tame; the oceans, fools and women.' Spiro T. Agnew (1970)

'A beautiful woman with a brain is like a beautiful woman with a club foot.' Bernard Cornfield (1974)

'It's not women's bodies that are the problem, it's their minds.' Steve Davies (1982).

And what must surely stand as a glowing monument to the understanding of women from the male point of view, is a remark delivered by an American judge during a rape trial during the late '70s: 'Women are sex objects whether they like it or not.'

If the general consensus of opinion above is anything to go

by, then women are basically mindless, deceptive, fickle creatures, fit only for the chores of the household or sitting pretty and silent beside their lord and master. The way this author has it, such utterances as quoted above, emanate only from the mouths of men who are unable to appreciate the feminine and responsive elements in their own psyche (something which we shall be looking at later). To say that all men are basically misogynists is a sweeping generalisation – clearly though, certain fundamental attitudes towards women are in serious need of reassessment. But how has the women's movement been dealing with this?

During the infancy of the present women's striving towards equality, the rest of the world looked on – some in sympathy, some in a state of ignorance – as feminists marched down streets bearing placards which read: 'Equal rights to jobs and education', 'The right to abortion', '24-hour child care', or 'Political power for women'. These petitions represented the fundamental issues to which they were objecting, like their identification with the servant of the family whose day was taken up by children and housework.

Eventually, the voice of the women's movement was heard and females began to assert their independence in business, politics, employment, in fact, in all strands of society, that had once been viewed as a rough, tough and competitive 'man's world'. However, this kind of emasculation, this female autonomy, brought problems in its wake. Many women carried their new found independence to the extreme and then discovered that they were missing something fundamental. Such fundamentals were the instinctive feminine need for love, children, home and family, even a 'man' about the house. The darling of the women's movement, Betty Friedan, expresses it thus: 'I think we must at least admit and begin openly to discuss the feminist denial of the importance of family, of women's own needs to give and get love and nurture, tender loving care.'

This throwing out of the baby with the bath water has created a great chasm which many women are now finding difficult to bridge: 'How can I burn the candle at both ends?' The candle is made up of equal parts of career independence and motherhood, and gives rise to dilemmas centred around family and marriage: 'How can I forge ahead in my career and still spend enough time with my children?' or: 'How can I be attractive enough to a man, when men are put-off by so-called career women?' These are only two of the dichotomies invoked by this new trend of the women's determination to make it in a man's world. What is surely required, and this applies no less to the male of the species, is an adaptation to this potentially stagnant situation, a look towards erasing the more stubborn stereotypes of what male and female roles are supposed to encompass. The momentum, I believe, is slowly gathering pace, a pace perhaps not fast enough for some of us. But the old habits die hard.

This gradual, collective reaction to the typical masks Male and Female are expected to wear is perhaps a crisis point in the understanding of ourselves and others on a large scale. The modern career woman, climbing the corporate ladder, and the house husband who discusses the price of baked beans in the supermarket, may, believe it or not, be perfectly suited to those stations in life. Whatever constraints or unkind labels are foisted upon the 'odd couple', whether we gossip in secret about the gay household across the road, consider the feminist movement a great joke or shun the newly-wed couple in the flat below because they are not of the same colour, one cannot escape the archetypal fact that human beings are drawn together. This happens often regardless of whether or not it is conventionally 'right' or 'wrong'. We see this in the modern world in the man whose new teenage wife shares the same taste in music as his teenage daughter; the woman who 'dates' married men; the guy who prefers older women, or indeed, the guy who prefers older men – a fact which even the irate audiences on American television's *Donahue* cannot erase.

Society's expectations of what a normal couple ought to resemble may be burdensome enough to the mismatched lovers, but it proves an even greater test to actually find that elusive partner in the first place. For some it resembles the quest of the hero discovering that apparently non-existent 'right one', and passively awaiting their arrival often seems as futile as the search itself. Perhaps the most obvious modern-day arenas where this ritualistic quest prevails are the night clubs and public bars of the weekend drinking set. One of its features occurs when some individual looks twice over his or her shoulder because they assume the handsome stranger in the corner to have 'noticed' them. It occurs when the fashionable young damsel (usually present with female cohort and half-lager) desires nothing less than some attractive stranger to walk over discreetly and 'chat her up', whilst simultaneously, said attractive stranger is wrestling with such internal conflicts as: 'Should I, or shouldn't I?', 'What will I say to her first?', or, 'What if she doesn't fancy me?'

On a broader level we find the Universal Quest embodied in the personal columns of provincial newspapers. Here, for the appropriate fee, one's outstanding virtues may be advertised in the hope of eliciting a reply from that Special Someone out there. A more recent extension of this phenomenon is in the growing number of limited companies marketing the idea that the Special Someone may be found waiting at the other end of a telephone line. It would appear that we are prepared to go to enormous lengths to discover that unique 'other', secretly awaiting us somewhere out there. Despite whatever methods we might employ, the search for the Eternal Enigma is something in which we all partake. Love lies at the root of this particular well worn path. I recall once standing in a busy 'fun pub' with my prematurely balding, bespectacled friend, casting glances around the prevailing scene of mini-skirted females and apprentice heart-throbs. We both surveyed this tinselled, plastic atmosphere, and my friend (who I was about to learn knew a thing or two about human nature) turned to me and remarked: 'You know what they're all looking for. They're looking for love.' His observation caused me to stop and think awhile.

A Study In Opposites

When Baudelaire remarked that we love women in proportion to their degree of strangeness to us, he made a discreet
allusion to the Universal Law of The Attraction of Opposites.
For whatever is felt to be different from us in the opposite sex
is somehow mysteriously captivating. The undeniable allure
possessed by the other points to this pre-existent fact in
nature; we are powerfully drawn, sometimes mesmerically,
to that which we do not possess. However, that Masculine
and Feminine are antithetical to each other is purely an
intellectual convenience. As nature has it, they are co-
partners, complements, and as such represent archetypal
forces emerging 'through' a suitable vessel. For example,
when the tabloid press speaks of 'maleness' it must utilise
adjectives such as 'dominant', 'courageous', 'forceful' and
'rugged'; qualities exemplified in such media heroes as
Rambo or Indiana Jones. Accustomed as we are to such
descriptions, they only refer to the masculine principle in
nature which (as is the nature of an archetype) only acquires
meaning and context when given expression by an appropriate vehicle.

The same situation applies to the contrasting female force,
as the energies of 'femaleness' are caught up within an actual
woman and lived out through their most natural medium of
expression. Thus, the feminine principle may be observed in
the 'soft', 'warm' and 'receptive' properties of such a woman,
as the nature of the archetype is embodied. However, it
would be erroneous to interpret these terms as being fundamentally derived from men and women themselves – they
are *a priori principles* rather than special qualities which
belong to the sexes.

The ancient Chinese sages paid due homage to this pair of
opposites in a graphic representation of masculine and feminine energy – namely the yang/yin symbol. The terms yang
(masculine) and yin (feminine) are thought, by scholars of
Oriental philosophy, originally to have meant, 'sunny' and

'sunless', alluding to the solar-type male 'spirit' and the lunar oriented female 'soul'. It is from the two Great Powers, according to traditional Chinese wisdom, that all creation arises. It would seem that male and female both contain properties which compel them to be attracted to each other, and – to paraphrase Jung – if there is any reaction, both are instantly transformed. Thus man and woman's essential attraction to each other is as natural and inescapable as the effect produced by the opposite poles of a magnet. Wherever the masculine force shall be embodied, so shall (as a pure consequence) the feminine be drawn to it. The positively charged pole of a magnet does not compel towards it a negative charge because of any desire on the part of the magnet. There is simply no resistance on either part. This is like saying that when a man eventually finds the 'right' woman, it cannot be attributed simply to his own hardy efforts for it must be asked, 'Who has attracted whom?'

These invisible forces manifest at all times in the world around us and lie not only at the fulcrum of human attraction; we may find them, for instance, permeating the structure of everyday language. For example, the yin phenomenon is suitably echoed when we speak of 'soft' lighting, 'gentle' colours, 'mellow' flavours and 'peaceful' moods. By way of contrast, the yang manifests in our descriptions, for example, of objects with 'hard' edges, 'sharp' features, 'bright' facings and 'clearly defined' characteristics.

These mental constructions which describe the covert behaviour of yin and yang are also used to illustrate the separate functions of the two 'halves' of the psyche. The conscious (yang) is masculine oriented since its mode of activity is ego discrimination, separating 'this' from 'that'; whilst the unconscious (yin) is generally feminine in nature, evaluating via the mysterious processes of intuition and feeling. The conscious mind is 'masculine' because it *actively* goes about classifying and making distinctions, whereas the preceptions of the unconscious are arrived at *passively*, i.e. without making the attempt to think. It is by observing the interplay of these mutually attracting forces, the outwardly rushing male spirit and responsive female matter, that one may lift away – if only for a moment – the veil which cloaks human affairs in so much mystery. These invisible energies have something to reveal about our modern relationships.

As a generalisation, men, in the first instance, are drawn to what is characteristically *physical* in a woman. The same, however, does not hold true for the woman since females tend to emphasise the less tangible properties of their opposite sex: personality, worldly success, power, intellectual prowess, and in particular, money making abilities. Hence, it transpires that the female psyche is oriented more by what the male 'does' than what he looks like, whilst the reverse may be said to be true for the masculine psyche. This unconscious arrangement is, I believe, caused by the intrinsic nature of the archetypes which permeate male and female psychology. On an abstract level one might apprehend it as the intangible, masculine force (spirit, energy) seeking its counterpart in the tangible, material entity of the feminine, hence towards a woman's body and physical characteristics. The feminine force (receptive matter) must draw upon itself the missing component of dynamic, male spirit which is *active*; thus the woman's accent is upon the male's achievements in the external world.

This interplay between male and female energies, mutually seeking one another in a partner, manifests concretely when a woman's heart skips a beat not because of his piercing blue eyes and manly chest, but because of his successful songwriting career and business savvy for striking profitable royalty deals. It manifests when a male is not in the least bit impressed by his woman's four 'A' levels and honours degree in Physics, but rather more interested in her dazzling, strawberry-blonde hair.

Blonde hair on a woman is a typical representation of what constitutes a turn-on for the male, perhaps also with long legs, and a shapely figure. Conversely, as has oft been noticed, a man does not have to be especially good-looking

31

for a woman to find him attractive, for she is unconsciously dealing with those pre-existent male 'intangibles' discussed in the previous paragraph, where worldly achievement must ultimately preside over physical qualities. As this is only the general rule of thumb, it cannot, and does not mean that women are never attracted by a handsome man or that the male population can never appreciate the mind of a woman. Rather, it indicates that the myriad descriptions of what one finds attractive in another – especially the ones we have hitherto discussed – are typical products of the way in which the sexes interact. These are in turn products of the spontaneous arrangements of yin and yang.

During the preparation of this book, I asked many of my friends, both male and female, if they could explain what it is they find particularly attractive in the opposite sex. Their responses to my survey were nothing like emphatic or clearly defined, which is what I had expected. However, the general consensus of opinion among females was that they would, eventually, have to settle for a partner who is going to be able to offer some kind of material *security*. This, taken on a symbolic level, points to the soft, mollient feminine seeking the containment of the masculine, for as the pure mountain stream descends the craggy mountain slopes and gathers in the nearest receptacle, together they will have formed a rock pool. However, symbolic pictures aside, women tend generally to gravitate towards that which will provide stability in a material sense, where some tangible evidence exists to demonstrate her security.

This phenomenon is perhaps a hangover from the days when man chased wild animals across frozen plains armed with primitive hunting weapons, and the female, presumably, awaited his return in order to prepare said food provisions, i.e. dead wild animal. Though this may sound exceedingly glib, it is a fact for many depth psychologists that we inherit the unconscious patterns of our ancestors. It is no less a fact that inner expectations about the warrior/husband venturing into the world to fight battles and bring home the prize, are etched upon the collective female unconscious. Though the warrior's quest in modern terms may mean nothing more hazardous than going out to work, doing battle with the rush-hour traffic and stopping off at the super-market *en route* home, Woman's expectation and image of Man as provider/supporter persists nonetheless.

The brittle, emancipated career woman may at first appear to be an exception to the rule, particularly when she can settle her own debts and raise two children singlehandedly. However, such abilities do not exclude her from deeply ingrained, unconscious assumptions about the role of the male sex in relation to the female. This syndrome does not apply only to women. Nor can it be 'blamed' on the individual; it is an *a priori*, collective archetype that has taken root in successive generations of human psychology. It is passed on down the line so that each man and woman bears the imprint of previous incarnations. The submissive qualities of women, for instance, that so enrage the feminist move-ment, are an intrinsic facet of the Historical Woman (the archetype). It would take literally hundreds of years to uproot Her. Moreover, the subjugation of the female in society is history's ignorant way of dealing with the feminine principle.

If woman's inherited image of man as furnisher of re-sources, warrior and strategist, is derived from instinctive patterns of male – female relating (I am considering here, the Stone Age epoch), then it figures that man's psychological genes must contain the image of woman as homemaker and provider of fleshly comforts. One only needs to recall the stereotyped picture of High-Powered, Overworked, Com-pany Executive arriving home to Pipe-and-slippers-at-the-ready-Wife to see how old archetypes die hard. If one aban-dons the modern technology, the three-piece suit and the time scale considerably, one finds High-Powered, Over-worked, Primitive Caveman worn out from a gruelling day's hunting as Attentive Cavewoman prepares something to eat with which to warm his world-weary bones. In modern settings, as I have mentioned, men's attraction to women has the emphasis laid mostly upon physical appearance; if a man's wife resembles a sexy Helen of Troy then she can be forgiven for her lack of intellect for he does not value it in her in the first place. This is not simply a case of men treating women as sex objects – the bête noire of the feminists – for this too is an outgrowth of our collective, psychological ancestry.

Within the arena of human relating, we are moved by a power far greater than the ego's, particularly when one considers our in-born expectations, erotic infatuations and compulsive, fatal desires. It is only when we begin to look deeper into ourselves, into our essential nature and the forces within, that some of our most sublime motivations begin to reveal themselves. Women do not simply look for security in the male because they are gold-diggers incapable of fending for themselves; nor can the male be realistically condemned for what is seen as his basic sex-mindedness.

The male's primary love of physical attractiveness represents an archetypal drive towards the unfathomable delicacy of the female; whereas the feminine force in nature, undifferentiated and formless, must attach itself to something solid and secure. Viewed on this level, one may glean that such mysterious forces as yin and yang possess a will of their own. We are, in one sense, merely vehicles for their expression. Perhaps it would be both wise and purposeful to try and discover what one's raging obsession really means. Why is it we must travel the lonely road in search of the Eternal Enigma as this impersonal spirit simultaneously pays no attention to our frustrations and despair? Why must we purposefully strive for something that can destroy and wreak emotional havoc, and still remain unaware of what it is that moves us? Could it be that the individual's plight to find love, and Eros's need to reveal himself through his eternal children, are one and the same?

CHAPTER 2

TAO AND TANTRA

TAO

The Chinese classic of philosophy, the *Tao Te Ching*, or the Classic of the Way and Power (attributed to Lao Tzu), stands as a remarkable testament to the profound depth and wisdom of the ancient Orient. It appeared in its final form somewhere between the sixth and fourth centuries BC, yet early Chinese philosophy attributes its real source to the Book of Changes, the *I Ching*, a perplexing system of divination using the varied formations of the yin and yang, written anywhere between 3000 and 1200 BC. As Heraclitus proclaimed in the West many years later, the *I Ching* holds that change is inherent within the cosmic order, that the universe exhibits an unending state of flux. It is the precarious dynamic tension between the two polar opposites that brings forth all creation.

On a human level, it is the dynamic imbalance between the respective natures of man and woman, their 'unalikeness', which ultimately brings them both together. Thus, the principles of Taoism have much in common with the nature of human attraction, personal relationships, and ultimately, with love itself. The essence of the Tao is ceaseless interplay between the poles of yin and yang, through which all manifestation arises; it therefore transpires that with the Tao there are no hard and fast rules. It is the course of something's unfolding, the manner in which nature (i.e. everything in the known universe) happens. Tao is not a thing or object in the specific sense; like love it is a process of becoming.

Taoism is a philosophy of life that is eminently practical despite its being charged with mysticism, as if it were some vacuous ideal with no reference whatever to the real world. These criticisms mostly stem from individuals steeped in the worldly consciousness of the material plane, unable to make rational sense of the paradoxes woven into the eighty-one chapters of the *Tao Te Ching*. It is ultimately pragmatic in that it reflects quite simply the ongoing processes of Man and the Universe, the unfolding of Nature from the great to the infinitely small. It peers into the inner world of man and woman, mirroring the complexities which arise from a mis-understanding of the machinations of the psyche and its body. For instance, it reveals man's perennial anxiety fostered by the Search for Security, the monumental task of attempting to function eternally with a peaceful mind. This is Man's great folly. The striving for security beckons insecurity because there is always something new to worry about. How many times does one hear of the wealthy person whose fear of poverty is in fact aggravated as his riches increase? Taoism would advocate seeing into these basic paradoxical truths in order to become disentangled from the web of confusion that is provoked whenever the mind is ignorant of itself.

This is one sense in which the Tao serves as a workable psychology. It is indeed impractical to embark upon a search for everlasting security because the universe is itself a rest-less creature. It is *insecure*. Hence, the Tao reflects our misun-derstanding of natural law. Its characteristic feature is the absence of a patriarchal god. For this reason it comes inti-mately close to the natural world. Like Zen Buddhism, it is concerned with pure experience, the realisation of one's inner psychic and physical processes and the most direct reality to which one can point.

The obscure way in which Tao has been defined seems to

suggest that it is fluid and inconstant in much the same way that love, having called upon the life of man, will vanish like some runaway phantom when an attempt is made to possess it. The Tao, like love, exhibits such an elusive quality when one attempts to 'get' it. To try to capture it is to misconstrue the nature of whatever it is one is striving to catch. Indeed, to 'get' Tao, or love for that matter, one must let go and allow it to enter of its own accord because it is always there and waiting to be discovered. For instance, in the exact same manner, when one wishes to relax, be creative, natural, spontaneous, there is simply no effort required. Likewise, to really see the person one loves, to glimpse some of their hidden nature, one must see without straining to look for anything, hear without necessarily listening for anything. Active listening and looking are subject to the often distorted interpretations of the ego. The creative unfolding of nature that is Tao is much like that force we call love. The following quotation from the *Tao Te Ching* echoes Oscar Wilde's maxim which says that a man will eventually kill the thing he loves: 'Whoever does anything to it will ruin it; whoever lays hold of it will lose it.' And we perpetually attempt to lay hold of it: just how many relationships have atrophied because one of the partners has proven to be over possessive?

And so, because of Tao's (and love's) formless enigmatic nature, existing in secret within the psyche, many poignant aphorisms, both ancient and modern, bear the stamp of paradox. Like the absurdity of the heart itself the following pieces of advice: 'When you don't seek, you find', and the Taoist, 'Adapt the nothing therein to the purpose in hand and you will have the use of the room', bear no relation whatever to the world of logical consistency. The Tao then, must be comprehended in terms other than logical; for example, the above sayings contain references to the mind's ability to act spontaneously and effectively yet seemingly without effort. Thus is the suggestion that the powers of mind are severely hampered by 'seeking' or too much interference from the intellect. The 'nothing' that is put to use refers not to the void of empty space, but to the stillness of mind. It is through this stillness, like allowing the ripples in a pool of water to become quiescent, that one acquires creativity. The result is a tremendous clarity and the harmonious balance between mind and body necessary for effective action. This kind of crystal clearness is none other than the purpose in hand. When such mental clarity prevails one will have full use of the room, as it cannot be grasped by the ego itself. Neither can love.

TANTRA

Further west, approximately four hundred years later, began another so-called philosophy of 'naturalness'. A collection of texts appeared in India which have since come to be known as the tradition of Tantra. Tantric thought is portrayed in images and ideas from the background of early Indian religion. It may perhaps be defined as a cult of ecstasy, a world affirming occult philosophy, a tradition encouraging the rapture of the emotions and empire of the senses. Many representations of Tantra appear in the form of highly emotive, erotic sculptures, depicting either mortals or deities in the act of sexual union. However, Tantric practices must not be misconstrued as a self-indulgent free-for-all, catering to the sexually promiscuous. The philosophy which underpins such acts is profound. Tantric rituals are devised as *symbolic* acts depicting the way in which the universe operates. It reveals the interplay and union of receptive/female and active/male energies, the eternal alternation between day and night forces, the yin and yang out of which all creation arises.

The name Tantra is derived from the Sanskrit word *tan* which means 'to weave'. The complete word Tantra has been taken to mean 'in the loom', with the allusion to the handiwork of the gods, the thread of life that is spun by Fate. From this no mortal may escape. In this context, Tantra may be seen as an attempt to come to terms with one's bodily, earthly existence, but the final aim of its teaching is along the same lines as Taoism: all manifestation in the universe is a consequence of the interplay of male and female forces. These forces are regarded as sexual in nature and all creation is imaged as the sexual union of the Divine Pair – hence the erotic sculptures. However, to place this issue of cosmic sexuality aside for one moment, in its most fundamental sense Tantra is a philosophy of life which always points to a deeper underlying reality than the one experienced on an everyday level. It points to the creative principle no less, that which seems to bring forth manifested events as if out of nowhere. And if this sounds vague, then consider it no different from the effects created by that which we now refer to as the unconscious mind.

In Tantra, the creative principle within the universe is considered sexual in nature. Thus the practice of prolonged sexual union has as its base the celebration of divine, pro-creative masculine and feminine energies. This act is dedicated to the deities Shiva and Shakti according to certain sources. It is through this ritualistic art that the Tantrika (one who practices Tantric love) seeks to arouse potent energies from within in order to arrive at a state of continuing physical and emotional harmony by delaying orgasm as long as possible: it is the original 'sex magick'. Sex magick is a specialised technique employed by the practising magician invoking powerful forces from within via the aid of sex. Though the idea may cause a few raised eyebrows in some corners of society, the philosophy behind it is ultimately pragmatic. At the moment of final orgasm, the ritual magician will release a powerful outlet of bio-physical energy, which when directed to the object of the ritual, acts as a potent attracting agent. There are less animalistic ways of performing a magical ceremony, but it cannot be denied that the release of sexual energies is a dynamic transforming agent, with or without Merlin's wand.

Just as our society frowns upon subjects which sound too resonant of the 'occult', so does it try to keep at bay – or at least under the counter – the more explicit, though natural aspects of human nature (quite necessarily in certain situations, where children are concerned, for instance). But as far as Tantra is concerned, sexual love engenders the ultimate state of being, the beautiful bliss of ecstasy by which one may transcend ordinary reality. Hence, the emphasis is not upon sexual arousal and physical sensation, but upon the profound and rich emotions invoked. The act of coupling is a catalyst for these feelings.

This rather serious approach has been necessary in order to contrast the underlying tenets of Tantric love with our present-day, often medieval, attitudes to sexual matters in the West. In areas of daily living we are, despite our contrived openness about the sexual arena, still fed with the assumption that sex is somehow naughty, obscene, dirty, taboo and a matter not to be discussed over tea and cucumber sandwiches with the vicar. When comedian Frankie Howerd joked about the Indian love text, the *Kama Sutra* as a 'Mrs Beeton's for sex maniacs', he echoed the West's trivialisation of something many of us inwardly fear or cannot comprehend in its deeper sense.

Our understanding of the sexual act is centred around the pursuit and achievement of orgasm, the final climatic release of energy. Tantric love is based on nothing of the kind. The objective is to prolong and perpetuate the sexual act in order to experience feelings of intense bliss, or as the Tantrika might have it, to share in the ecstasy of Shakti and Shiva's divinity. In contrast, the West's de-humanising of sex has seen its apotheosis in 'scientific' research on sexual partners. Here the responses and stimuli are neatly catalogued and detailed by the attending staff who (to quote astrologer Stephen Arroyo) 'have all these people screwing around in their laboratory'. To the Tantrika, lovemaking is a deeply personal issue, where the individual is the centre for the flow of sensual feeling, for the emergence of the creative energies of the universe. Love is not something to be performed over a laboratory table whilst the earnest statistician makes notes in his book. Typically, many individuals regard the phenomenon we call love as something to be 'had', as if it were an objective 'thing' out there: to the Tantrika and Taoist, the 'out there' does not exist. The universe, and all of its potent energies are also oneself.

However, modern man's unceasing attempts to lay claim to love, despite this being a contradiction in terms, is intimately bound up with what we call security, the security of having someone's love. In this way, the ego remodels the outer world to suit its own devices and demands from the partner, 'love' as its own, safe possession. It may not occur to such a person that such insistencies plant the unconscious seed of discontent in the other. Were he (or she) to relax this demand, that love might actually be offered freely by the partner. This clinging to life and love carries beneath it a layer of mistrust and insecurity. If we would willingly let the reigns go more often, then life, love and the creative power of the Tao would flow. We would avail ourselves of the use of the room.

The Tao of Love
I
Like Tao, love is not an object
It is a way of becoming.
You cannot just take hold of it;
For in trying to do so, like the air around you,
It will evade your grasp.
Slip through your fingers.

Tao contains all opposites, yet of itself has none.
Wherever the masculine stretches forward,
The feminine must follow close behind.
Wherever he goes she will always be.
Cast as his shadow.

But Tao who is behind this Great Polarity,
Draws nothing unto itself.
Does not change; though it is change.

Has no meaning; though it is meaning.
Possesses no shape; though it is shape.

For what Tao is can only be experienced,
And only then, when mind is in harmony with its body;
When body is in harmony with its world.
Likewise, love is to be; not to have.
Love is to do; not a word, a thing.
This is called the way of Nature,
The essence of the Tao.

II
Let go of Tao and it shall come to you,
Likewise do the same to love.
Now and then let go of someone,
And they shall return to you,
Without seeking, one finds.

To follow the changing seasons is Tao.
When it is correct action to move swiftly,
Then one must do precisely that.
When it is correct action to travel slow,
One must adapt in accordance.
But no one can tell you when.

Like Tao, love appears perplexing.
When our relationships appear secure and still,
Something often happens;
Like the full garden overcome by weeds;
Or calm waters preparing for a storm.
This is typical of the way.

III
It is said the path of love runs not smoothly;
So is it with humans.
And human love beholds many changes;
Spirited at first, maybe stagnant afterwards.
What travels must come to rest;
That is Tao, neither one nor the other.

Yet it is in man's loneliest hour,
In the bleak onslaught of suffering,
That we hear the familiar cry of pain.
And the more he would hold on tight,
The less would he become.
To be full again, he must first become empty.

And then at first, without wisdom,
In his lonely phantom world,
He may stretch too far;
Strive too hard;
For too long.
Yet if he shall let go,
In him shall Tao be restored.

Between the worlds of Yin and Yang,
Meaning may be found.
Though not in only the one event,
It shall be seen in the whole course of them.
Should one turn to look within,
And face oneself.

IV
Giving up effort is not without struggle,
Though trying too hard is easy.
Opening your heart, or stressing your opinion;
Which one is the most facile?

Learn how to become a vessel;
How to allow the watery depths to become still.
That is how one shall see clearly;
How one shall love from within.
Dissolve your false images of others;
Tao is seeing clearly, behaving accordingly.

On occasion we must be cruel to be kind,
Intervening with the correct action.
But the masculine's reach must not exceed its grasp,
For it sows discord in our relationships.
We must return to the feminine,
To Tao's fine art of balancing.

V
If you are loved is it not for its own sake?
When Tao is practised one takes no thought.
If you love do you ask for recompense?
Tao provides yet asks for nothing.
When true understanding occurs, the people do not beg for love,
Being complete in itself, Tao does not demand from them.

Your loved one is a mirror placed before you;
An image which cannot disappear.
But do not strain the eyes,

For that way you will never see it.
Do not look about you for a reflection,
For it is the one looking which contains it.

The principle of attraction is everywhere.
It is freely exerted;
It is spontaneous.
Subject to Tao, it cannot escape it.
Within it one is an indivisible part,
Belonging to those we meet every day.

VI
Tao is a principle through which creation occurs.
This too lies beneath human action.
Whilst laughing aloud, one must prepare for silence;
Whilst crying tears, one may expect next to smile;
Whilst practising humility, a little arrogance must be forthcoming.

VII
As for the man and woman who drip spite for each other,
To the Tao this is perfectly natural.
If they did not come together in such enmity,
It would not be Tao.

As soon as one sees oneself, Tao will be present,
Then clever scrutiny of others will disappear;
The ones we call husband or wife.
For whilst this is happening, a shadow is cast;
The shadow of one's own crooked opinion.
Can one point the finger at others without the use of the hand?

VIII
All that we may speak of with any clarity,
Is that one segment called the Now.
For now is part of the Process,
That now knows not.
Like the air in winter, love may grow cold;
Though we shall not suspect it in the heat of summer.
Yet being here now is to partake of the Great Process.

One may call this process Tao,
Yet it must be seen with open eyes;
Being so great, infinitely long;
One cannot perceive whence it began.
For it is futile to ask of its beginning,
And at which point it should end.

CHAPTER 3

THE ASTROLOGY OF LOVE

One often detects the faint twinkling of fear in those who proclaim the unreality of nature's oldest and most reliable oracle. It is as if the mention of the word 'astrology' is an offense to hard earned twentieth-century logic. Nevertheless, one ought to expect the old ego barriers to rise when speaking of such nonsense, for it *is* nonsense, if only in that the parallels between the planetary motions and the events in one's life, do not make any plausible sense to the intellect. The correlation simply does not exist. I have given up the vain attempt to convince astrological atheists of the validity of this subject, for they continually insist: 'The facts, where are the facts?' and I stand defeated. It is ineffective to point out to them that one can only experience astrological truths directly as a matter of *personal* fact. That kind of defence must seem so much like a cop out.

Yet the new physics is turning the world of impersonal science into something very personal indeed. Where observations are made in sub-atomic realms, objective 'facts' crumble into non-existence. Objectivity dies in these sophisticated experiments since it has been revealed that the results of certain experiments are dependent upon the attitudes and expectations of the observer. Thus, instead of arriving at definite, objective conclusions, whilst attempting to measure the nature of the universe, the experimenter observes his relation towards it, or in the words of one of the giants of modern physics, Werner Heisenberg, he 'encounters himself'. If we broaden this microcosmic view to that of the macrocosm, it confirms that one's world view is coloured by the inner subjective world.

One's outer environment is shaded ever so subtly by the pigments emanating from the inner self. That is, not only do we view the world *our* way (logical enough, I hear you say), but what comes back from that world to enter our lives, i.e. events, chance, misfortune, is a manifestation of that original, often unconscious world view.

Astrology proves to be an invaluable aid in revealing the individual's general, psychological outlook. However, with traditional horoscopy we are back to the land of the story book, in a world populated by symbolic centaurs, fishes, water-bearers and heavenly twins: archaic terminology; ancient Roman divinities and a mandala depicting a map of the heavens. Yet we have ventured into precisely the same territory as depth psychology, with its expositions on the archetypes, in particular those of yin and yang, which we have discussed as an archetypal pair of opposites permeating the psyche. As we have seen, it is from these two great elemental powers that the universe arises.

We have the ancients to thank for conceiving of the blueprints to which these energies will conform, or, said another way, illustrating the way in which humans make use of the psychological energies placed at their disposal. Those energies 'appear', albeit in symbolic form, on an individual's birth chart. One of the horoscope's fundamental building blocks lies in the symbolism of the four elements, Fire, Earth, Air and Water. These are derived from the underlying principles of the masculine yang and feminine yin. Thus two Great Powers beget four elements: Fire and Air, in keeping with the nature of yang, and Earth and Water, which constitute the substance of yin. We may hear of a 'fiery' individual, a fellow who is 'down to earth', a 'light and airy' temperament, or a 'still-waters-run-deep' type, whilst unconsciously referring to the archetypal forces of which such folk are the living symbol. If we may utilise models to portray the inner symbolism then we may reasonably construct examples in order to depict the interaction between them, for one is understood in terms of the other, and vice-versa.

There are four elements divided among twelve signs, three signs share the nature of one particular element: Fire signs: Aries, Leo and Sagittarius; Earth signs: Taurus, Virgo and Capricorn; Air signs: Gemini, Libra and Aquarius; and the Water signs: Cancer, Scorpio and Pisces. It is in denoting such elemental correspondences that we may observe the primal archetypes at work, and on our familiar everyday level make use of certain common adjectives. For example, we may describe the Fire type as active, energetic, wilful, volatile; the Air type as 'light', restless, breezy, freedom-loving; Earth as stable, enduring, solid, supportive; Water as fluid, changeable, deep, reflective.

In a figurative sense, the four elements also occupy the human psyche, and the individual to whom we attribute the qualities of Fire, for instance, embodies that universal principle. Yet that same individual will carry also, to varying degrees, the energies associated with the other primal elements. Indeed, our fiery subject will display qualities that are not at all considered a fundamental attribute of Fire. Nonetheless, an individual will tie his view of reality to one main, dominant function of consciousness, thus stems the efficacy of our elemental typology. Where Fire predominates in the most obvious manner, Earth – as its polar opposite – is relegated to the unconscious and as such is an unfamiliar, unexpressed quantity. Similarly, when Air directs the main focus of consciousness, the opposing – though complementary – attributes of Water naturally fall into disuse in the darkness of the inner self. But as one cannot be too specific in this area, or too general for that matter, the following presentation stands in the mid-ground between the sublime art of astrological interpretation and the somewhat dubious system of sun-sign compatibilities and incompatibilities. Let us first then, look at the Fire – Earth polarity.

The ultimate Fire principle is echoed in the folk maxim, 'it is better to travel hopefully, than to arrive'. In it one finds a philosophy of life that guides almost all of the Fire person's actions. However, as befits the way of nature, wherever one energy appears so too must its opposite. Thus Earth, symbolising the force of inertia, physicality, solid matter and states of rest (hence its polarity with the restless, energetic spirit of Fire), is suggested in the 'arriving'. 'Better to travel' alludes to Fire's enthusiasms for the present moment, the possibilities which lie in the future and the *ideal* picture that lies in his head. This love of the ideal, as one might expect, permeates his attitude towards relationships. In contrast to his Earth counterpart, Fire often feels let down when he does 'arrive'. Then he is required to attend to stark, monochrome reality and the facts and details of everyday living, something with which Earth has little trouble. The Earth type likes to know what lies beyond that symbolic road into the future, to have already 'arrived'. Earth seeks to be securely prepared for the rainy day that often never comes (to Earth, anyway) whereas Fire is usually happy to live for the moment. For Fire, this does not indicate a lack of concern for what happens tomorrow, it is simply that he doesn't feel the need to be 'armed' with definite, strategic plans for the future. His faith in himself is sufficient to get him there. Earth's love of security and tangible reality, if carried to extremes, will slide him into a materialist's rut. He will be unable to picture the road ahead, will be consequently devoid of any appreciation of the changes which may lie beyond today. Fire though, is usually already there, in spirit, at least.

With the elements of Air and Water we enter into the field of relationships proper. These principles appear to belong more to the world of human relating than do Fire and Earth, which may be considered as universal 'first' principles. I say this because Fire, as a metaphor for the spark of life, or that which ignites the spirit in all living beings, and Earth, as the symbolic container, the physical vessel which carries that spirit, precede the true birth of the thinking and feeling man. Hence, it is with Air and Water that life becomes fully humanised. The entity has acquired the gift of thought, communication and speech, and eventually becomes an emotional being with an appreciation of feeling values. I must apologise for perhaps sounding a little high brow and waxing symbolic. To always describe someone purely in terms of external action is effective only if a vacuum exists beneath the ego surface and nothing else can be held to account for their outward behaviour. Thus if we are genuinely to understand others, we must dig to the very roots of what makes them what they are, and (if you will pardon the dire analogy) astrology is a useful spade.

Lying at the roots of Air and Water are the contrasting principles of left-brain (logical) thinking, with its products of analysis, reason, compromise, moral issues, etc., and right-brain (intuitive) feeling, giving rise to the creative process, imagination, the 'sixth-sense', and emotional evaluation. This dyad is also connected with the elements of Fire and Earth: Fire, arriving at its deductions intuitively and spontaneously, shares some of its world view with Water; and Earth, who must form a sound and logical picture of reality, is close to Air when viewed in this context. The prime difference between Air and Water thus lies in a kind of irreconcilable subject/object oriented picture of the world. Air must forever insist upon making objective sense of whatever he experiences, whether it be an abstract mathematical equation, the problem of the creation of the universe, or the absurd heart of the human being. Water, by contrast, usually feels little need to reach out into the sphere of external facts and details in order to clothe himself with a view of reality. His intuition tells him all he needs to know. Water lives for the world of feeling, effortlessly able to perceive what is happening beneath the surface of others, and blessed with an intuitive talent that is sadly underestimated in modern society. To say that it 'feels right' to do something (and it literally does not matter what the action) apparently displays an aberration of logic.

This is precisely how Air is likely to regard the ephemeral

expressions of the Water type. There is so much to be reconciled between this often warring pair of opposites. Air, whose *raison d'être* is operating in life via clearly defined principles wrought with the dissecting knife of the intellect, can rarely comprehend the essentially feeling-toned consciousness of Water. The convention of logic cannot be applied to the ebb and flow of tides of feeling.

The following light-hearted look at relationships is essentially an observation of the way in which the elements behave within individuals. It portrays the likely outcome manifested by their various combinations. The accounts do not refer exclusively to either sex, nor are they merely concerned with sun signs. They denote the patterns engendered in relationships with a clear emphasis of that element in the individual's psychological make-up.

Fire Meets Fire

Like most good romantic novels, this relationship equates to a twentieth-century Romeo and Juliet (i.e. its characteristic passions). It begins quite naturally with thoughts of living happily ever after, for Fire partners are seeking the 'ideal', exciting relationship. The very principle of romance itself could well be attributed to the element of Fire. The opulent settings and explicit glamour it suggests are far removed from the more mundane aspects of mortal life. Fire often bears a palpable grudge towards the details of harsh, black-and-white reality.

To keep it truly alive, Fire requires the kind of effervescent activity in relationships that would wear out the sober, taciturn type. A Fire–Fire partnership is characterised in the colloquial expression 'never a dull moment'. One might indeed describe this partnership as volatile. If it engenders a rather healthy, creative tension where both partners provide a stimulus for each other, then the dynamo can continue to burn brightly. However, I think it safe to declare that one would witness the occasional but inevitable moments of fury caused by bruised egos; Fire people do rather tend to like getting their own way and occupying the main focus of attention, just a little. This can pose one small problem though, for there can only ever – literally – be *one* centre of attention, and both partners here inexorably claim the right to be 'it'.

At least here is one relationship unlikely to succumb to the cancer of boredom or the exaltation of humdrum trivialities bound up in the fabric of existence. They are too concerned with the whole of life's picture to notice the small details which comprise it. Affection, for instance, will be expressed liberally and generously since the emotional life of Fire possesses an ebullience and exuberance, in contrast to the more tender approaches of Water. The dynamism in the nature of Fire means that they can openly give affection without having to lean too much on the 'heavy' button. That, they leave to the Water types.

In each discussion of the elements under consideration, I will attempt to pinpoint the main areas of difficulty experienced as a result of the particular pairing. In the instance of Fire-Fire, they are created by self-centredness and an unwillingness regarding give-and-take, or indeed, no conception whatever of compromise. If there may, at any one time, be only one focal point of attention, then consequently the attention demanded by Fire may be unforthcoming from a Fire partner, for, of course, it works both ways. Fire does not demand of others in any other way. When their well-intentioned advances are met with icy reproach, one then witnesses the child-like feelings of Fire, truly upset that a world could be so full of disdain and insensitivity. Nevertheless, they can soon find someone else to appreciate them, or so they believe.

Fire Meets Earth

We have already observed a typical metaphor for this diametrically opposed pair of elements. Here is what occurs in a typical male-female relationship. If the male is the Earth partner, then he is unconsciously seeking the 'absent' Fire component in his conscious make-up: spontaneity, vision, a sense of meaning, and a more expansive feel for life. Dare I say it, he is looking for this in his woman. If Earth lies in the female partner, she possesses an abundance of practical wisdom and the capacity for the common sense aspects of everyday routine. She is thus looking for a diversion from her twilight world, and will look to the male to increase the tempo of her life. This pull of opposites is what draws the utterly conventional and perhaps self-effacing female (Earth), to the often non-conformist, ebullient and dynamic male (Fire), as the unconscious, unlived-out halves of the male and female are brought together.

The prudent and ever-so-realistic Earth person is fascinated by the genial candour and spiritedness of Fire. Should they come together in a relationship, Earth nurtures the belief that Fire is the ticket to a more enriching, meaningful existence. Fire is fond of dramatic expressions and somewhat explicit theatricals in order to release his ego energies. *This is precisely what Earth has been waiting for*. As the relationship develops, Earth anticipates settling into the proverbial lasting partnership. He must apply his notion of security to whatever he experiences. Since Earth is the archetypal 'builder', most happy with the tangible evidence of his own diligent labour, he is likely to graft his expectations of permanence and solidity on to something which cannot always be subject to permanent and reliable foundations. Earth likes the reassurance of constancy, and to know that the same pleasurable experience can be repeated over again; Fire loves change and often does not, or indeed cannot, conceive what he will be doing until the moment presents itself.

Fire will often marvel at the way in which Earth makes a splendid job of attending to his daily routine, manages to keep a cool head in a crisis and, with effortless calm, finds solutions to the most vexing of mundane problems. However, there is often a resistance to these mundane aspects of the Earth temperament that makes Fire inwardly want to scream. Fire lives and breathes for the moment, whereas Earth tends to enclose experience into little containers, allotting a certain amount of time to duty, relaxation, pleasure etc. Earth generally attempts to *construct* a secure future by his meticulous and so often over-careful planning. However, it would not be unfair to point out that the *typical* expression of this element is perhaps a little dull and sterile, an opinion fostered because Earth is underrated in social encounters.

If Earth is trying to 'secure' a relationship with Fire, the life is imperceptibly sucked out of it and Fire becomes bored and restless, endlessly complaining about sameness and routine. This can stimulate the explosive qualities of the Fire person, resulting in cloaked anger and irritability, although he (or she) may be unaware of precisely what is happening. Consequently, Earth will either attempt to contain such eruptions, or be completely repulsed by them. This is one symptom of the unconscious vicious circle now propelled into motion. Earth starts to believe that Fire is an irresponsible child; Fire is inwardly convinced that Earth is slowly draining the life out of him. If neither of them can come to terms with the warring opposites within, the unconscious will intervene and yet another 'ideal' relationship will bite the dust.

Fire Meets Air

Among the many elemental combinations this one is considered a favourable augury. In a sense they need each other. If Fire is to be permitted free reign for his future aspirations, and to express his innate faith in himself as fully as possible, he requires Air as a stimulus, and to occasionally bring him back down to earth level. Whereas the elements of Earth and Water may despair of Fire's animated and irreverent persona, Air may simply encourage it. Similarly, if Air is to advance his intellectual theories and opinions without losing sight of the human factor, he needs Fire to infuse a certain warmth into his fundamentally impersonal approach.

A relationship between Fire and Air requires, for it to thrive, a busy social life, a varying of interests and 'change', the keyword to the success of such a combination. Air and Fire will require much breathing space of their own, and both partners may take quite a while before deciding on such a commitment as marriage or living together. In the first instance, there is little true inner depth in either element, so that neither experiences the painful little moments so often evoked by an absence of the partner. Whenever Fire is feeling dispirited his method of release is to make fun of the situation. However, the fiery individual is only depressed for so long as his gregarious soul will permit it. Air, in such a situation, calls upon his natural propensity for Mr Spock type logic and rationalises those feelings, for depression is a virus, and an illogical one at that.

Disagreements are apt to manifest whenever Fire embarks upon an idealistic new venture which Air thinks of as too lofty and selfish. Air consequently refuses to pay homage to the partner's rather large ego which, after all, is larger than Air's. Even though Air compromises much better than Fire, he makes no issue of the restless human spirit and uniqueness of the individual, the outpouring of which is Fire's true vocation. Thus Fire is often accused by Air of being 'selfish', since Air is what one might term the most 'socially oriented' of the elements. Air will often tailor his actions to those favoured by the prevailing group, hence his adaptability. What he consistently fails to realise is that what is good for the group may not bode well for certain individuals. Someone is not necessarily 'selfish' – with all of its shameful connotations – when they do not wish to 'join in with the rest of us'.

If there is too little Earth or Water in both partners' psychological make-up, the relationship will possess an abundant source of enthusiastic, lively interaction. Yet the centre will be almost a vacuum devoid of substance. Fire and Air people are more attuned to the outer *appearances* of relationships, placing an awful amount of emphasis upon the gloss of what is currently in vogue. And their general novelist's eye-view of the world, plus some considerable eager curiosity about life, ensures that they are just as much interested in their neighbour, or the people sitting opposite, as they are in each other. Air in particular has more 'buddies' than close friends and will usually begin a relationship on the keep-your-distance-until-I've-figured-you-out principle. Indeed, Air will test the water of a potential relationship before becoming immersed (if that is the appropriate term). The consequence of this is many and numerous 'short' affairs, which when viewed from afar resemble an obsessional collector's mania. At least with a Fire partner Air will be kept busily occupied attempting to figure out a partner who is not so uncomplicated as he at first appears.

Fire Meets Water

The heady combination of these two elements can, and does, produce some explosive moments laden with eddying passions and emotional complexities. Both of these elemental types are possessed of powerful emotions which must find an effective release; the lordly passions of Fire follow the path of extroversion and easily infect others around him; by contrast Water's feelings are withdrawn into the inner world and often engulf him to such an extent that he cannot easily disrobe of the emotional overcoat he has deemed fit to wear. Both of them are at their best when living on an emotional peak, and when these feelings are shared mutually there exists a state of joy which only the knowing heart can comprehend and meaningfully translate.

In either type, the orientation towards the outside world is firmly smeared with a subjective bias. Both are apt to make as a focus of consciousness, the 'human' factor, in contrast to the more analytical and pragmatic way of viewing reality. For instance, Fire demonstrates its need for creative ego release, and Water harbours sure instincts about the inner natures of others and is sensitive enough to be able to comprehend their needs. As depth psychology describes it, the perceptions of Fire and Water stem from an unconscious process best described as intuition, or what the academics might define as 'right brain' evaluation. Thus we have in both elemental types an artistic temperament: creative, changeable, sensitive, irrational. In contrast, the attitudes of Earth and Air are essentially rational and reality oriented. These similarities are why I consider Fire to be a better match for Water than most traditional texts on astrology would have us believe. Certainly it is easier than the Fire–Earth or Air–Water combinations.

On good days, the warm spark and cheeriness of Fire opens up a channel for the response of Water, kindling feelings of vigour and excitement in the watery individual. Fire is quite naturally skilled at precipitating such enthusiasms. What seems to be missing is a little subtlety, and the undervalued gift to be truly passive and contemplative. The picture begins to develop a fault when Water turns the entire performance over to Fire, leaving him with the responsibility for the other's happiness and contentment. Of course, Fire is at first only too pleased to assume the mantle of lover/entertainer, though in time the unconscious demands from a watery partner may prove too 'heavy'. Yet even though Fire has a lot to give of himself, too little may be donated to the relationship.

Water, often to his detriment, erects his value system solely upon the emotional experiences derived from a close relationship. With Fire, he is in danger of getting his fingers burned by perhaps contemplating too smooth a ride. The outspoken and often erratic expressions of Fire register in the watery consciousness as insensitivity, in some cases brutality. Then the moment arises when Water begins to feel rejected. When Water's feelings are hurt they are felt more deeply and acutely than any other element. Moreover, they pass unvoiced, which is when the real conflict begins. Unsurprisingly, Fire begins to withdraw emotionally from the relationship. With his innate intuition he senses that the shadows of resentment are at large within the partner, especially in relation to his very open and candid expressions. Water though, does not necessarily appreciate these 'candid expressions', and considers that a sledgehammer just might have the edge in subtlety and tact.

Fire, on his part, can barely understand what it is that causes someone to withdraw into brooding behaviour to such an extent. If repelled far enough, Fire will move his attentions elsewhere, a portent that the relationship is fast becoming superfluous to requirements. In relating to one another, Fire and Water need to become more aware of their 'missing halves': Fire must develop patience, thoughtfulness, and trouble himself to take a closer look at the sensitivities of others. Water, by contrast, must on occasion stand back to see that the world is in fact much larger than he can readily appreciate. Water carries an invisible 'keep out' notice to safeguard against anything he fears may intrude upon his private world.

Earth Meets Earth

Earth is so finely attuned to the established status quo, the security of material comforts and the needs of his body, that the physical world becomes virtually a shrine at which to worship. Needless to say, making graven images of the emblems of stability and fiscal security tends to limit one's vision. Such 'reality' orientation tells only half a story of the *real* world. The *real* world to the Earth type usually consists of nothing more than the way in which it simply appears. Earth has little patience with the finer abstractions which go to make up the universe. This leaves the earthy pair with some prosaic values about the way life 'is', and what a relationship ought to constitute.

An Earth partnership usually contains the requisite ingredients for durability. The earthy pair, often despite all else, will attempt to make things *last*. This element usually values all of the conventional forms of courtship, the engagement ring, expensive (designer label) presents and, eventually, the time-honoured church wedding. Despite their conservative exterior, Earth types have a considerable penchant for the pleasures of the flesh, for although they may be reluctant to demonstrate physical affection outdoors (as it were), sensuality is one of the keywords ascribed to the element of Earth. Indoors may be another matter entirely; sex for Earth is often a ritualised affair, suggesting a layer of deeper significance to lovemaking for them than just the 'usual'. However, they are inclined to repress the emotional sides of their natures, and Earth is often at pains to truly let go and open up. The sexual act offers them the opportunity to release some of their unconscious carefree selves.

It is precisely this carefree element which is conspicuously absent from Earth-Earth relationships. The structure upon which they would found their lives is rarely permitted to change shape. This translates as a constant repetition of the way in which they have fashioned their lives, since familiar experience often means security. The partner is expected to conform to this pattern also (and here we encounter Earth's notorious possessive streak – they simply get used to the other person being there). They require the assurance that they can rely upon the partner to be in a certain place at a certain time. This is fortunate for the Earth relationship, for each possesses an inbred sense of loyalty and duty that somehow compels them to adjust to routine. Fire types, on the other hand, would be steered to insanity by such matters.

The unexpected is often a threat to Earth because change is only a feature of their hidden, unconscious selves. If Earth partners are married with children, their offspring may bear the brunt of the parents' unlived out natures. It is not uncommon to discover earthbound parents despairing with the volatile temperament of rebellious and bohemian, though highly creative, sons and daughters. In like manner, one discovers the grown up children of Water-type parents responding to them in a cool, distant, even contemptuous manner. This insists that the parent keeps safely at arms length. It is all that the 'child' can do to negate the feeling of being sucked back into the parental womb.

The 'problem' which underpins the Earth relationship is the consequence of too much rootedness in security and routine. The relationship thus acquires an inevitable blandness and sterility, though Earth may not view this as especially problematic. Indeed, the realisation may never dawn to Earth that he is in a rut. The more he clings to his securities, the more will the outside world apparently threaten to dislodge the heel so firmly entrenched in the ground. After all that tenacious planning and hard effort too! However, Earth-Earth is a good portent, if only because they ask the same things of life and happen to be tracing the same steps towards the future. This is the archetypal old-fashioned relationship based on values of loyalty, protection, hard work, monetary stability, the hearth and home.

Earth Meets Air

The elements of Earth and Air share many kindred features. Both seek life's truths in the external, objective world where everything requires a reason, and must generally conform to intellectual criteria. Earth structures its reality in accordance with whatever material is at hand. Its ultimate concern is with what will 'work'. A relationship that works for Earth is one driven by the faithful wheels of security and dependability, whereas Air's soul seeks the ever-widening range of experience, which may only be reached from above ground level. Air cannot rest his attentions upon one area for long and must be sufficiently detached from the more mundane aspects of life. Earth, however, is essentially rooted in the world of form. In this, despite their inherent similarities, we find the basis of their differing modes of operation.

It is likely to be the Earth type who becomes more deeply involved on a feeling level, even though he is apt to cast a cautious eye upon the world of human emotion. When Earth decides to form a commitment in a relationship it is with a view to building a future fashioned from the bricks and mortar of the real world. Earth excels in its capacity for turning hopes and dreams into reality. As Earth is symbolic of the physical world, then it consequently finds a miniature replica in the physical body itself. This means that the earthy type is powerfully attuned to the senses, the requirements of the body. Earth is thus happy with whatever is palpable, whatever he or she can touch, see or feel. In relationships, the Earth type often exhibits a rather uncomplicated, warm sensuality, even passion, which may belie his outwardly conservative manner.

On the other hand, Air is more fond of the 'prettier' aspects of human relating, born from his intellectual contrivance of what is 'pleasant' and 'nice'; the gentle, almost reluctant kiss on the cheek, a single rose perhaps, or a tastefully written love letter ornamented with articulate gestures. The comparison is drawn because Air is not quite such a 'touching' person as is his Earth partner and often completely undervalues the language of touch. Moreover, Air does not require the expressions of physical sensation to prove that the other person still cares. He stays clear of emotional matters too. For instance, if Air were to leave the logical world behind and fall in love, then 'abnormally possessed' might well serve as an apposite description. Yet the air temperament does well to avoid irrational feeling. When it descends upon him, he is at its mercy. Nothing is more bewildering to Air than the rush of nebulous, not to say incalculable, emotion.

Despite Earth's quiet warmth and gentleness, it tends to lack the effervescence of Air in social encounters. The latter is noticeably adept at casual conversation and this kind of spontaneity comes second nature. Some of the more talkative Air types make use of verbal silliness in the social arena; both partners are dining out for instance, and Air remarks, 'Isn't this meal just delish'?' (delicious), as Earth closes his eyes in disbelief at what he has just heard. However, Earth secretly comes to admire Air's animated way of communicating, though finds less to appreciate in his penchant for intellectual theorising, unless of course, it is of some immediate, practical value. These elements can combine well in this respect, for Air's mental drawer of dissociated facts and figures can find a useful vehicle in the hands of the realistic Earth type.

The most common dividing line between Earth and Air as modes of operation has already been referred to: Earth's requirement for security which so often turns to possessiveness and exacerbates the fear of losing what one has acquired. A partner of Earth's is often regarded as a possession. This in turn draws upon jealousy, and if exhibited in sufficient quantities by Earth, Air will chafe against such 'heaviness', or perhaps find an excuse to leave.

Earth Meets Water

Rather like the Fire–Air relationship, temperaments containing the qualities of Earth and Water are often a harmonious blend since they assist in complementing one another. However, as with any other mixture of personalities, this relationship bears its seed of disharmony; here most often in the time honoured 'container'/'contained' syndrome whereby one of the partners acts fundamentally as a receptacle, provider for, and supporter of the other. The 'contained' is usually blissfully unaware of the concerns of the outside world for so long as he or she may be centred and clothed in the love of the other. The partner looking to be contained is quite often the Water type. This may engender negative repercussions if Water becomes too comfortable in the solid surroundings of Earth. It will weaken what was hitherto a reliable and supportive foundation.

In human terms this means that Earth finds it difficult to deal with the emotional demands of a watery partner. The realistic, pragmatic psychology of Earth cannot fully comprehend, much less appreciate, the shifting currents of emotion which meander through the psyche of the Water type. Earth is apt to dismiss this as overt sensitivity or simply asks Water what is the matter with him. To complicate matters further, Water cannot really produce an open, straightforward answer. Earth comprehends the universe in a simplistic, linear fashion, preferring black to be black, and white to be white; Water detects the subtle shadings of grey which allow one object to merge imperceptibly into another, appreciates how surface appearances often belie the inner reality. Despite these differences in outlook, Earth is a good partner for the Water person. Moreover, Water is not threatened in the same way as he is by Fire or Air, and for his part manages to round off some of the hard edges of 'realism' with which Earth often becomes encrusted.

A love relationship to the Earth and Water types means a feeling of deep-rooted security, like so many lonely travellers on a hostile road who eventually find their way home. The quality of Water's love is that of compassion, the ability to nurture, and the instinctive response to another's emotional needs. This is almost indistinct from Earth's protective and supportive way of demonstrating their love. These elements are associated with the roots and matrix out of which an entity must grow. Thus Earth and Water often exhibit super-conventional attitudes towards family matters. They inherit the values fostered by their parents. Even in the 'new age', traditional values regarding relating – the institution of marriage for one – are ingrained in the consciousness of Earth and Water, particularly those of loyalty and protection. Earth and Water serve as the custodians of all that has been supportive during the growing years, retaining an intimate fondness for the past. Consequently, their instincts are to acquire and arrive at a sense of belonging, both to the past which shaped them, and the partner in the here and now.

Water is apt to feel that Earth is often unresponsive to its more subtle moods. This is because Earth has little time for ambivalence and once an opinion is formed, is unlikely to seek further clues to the changeable nature of the Water type. The compensation is that Earth can help Water to be more realistic. Certainly Water must make the effort, if he is to adapt creatively to a relationship with Earth. On the other hand, Water can assist in the process whereby Earth can see life from a different perspective, where black is not always quite so black, and white not always so white.

Air Meets Air

It becomes almost a binding necessity for the Air types to be free from routine encumbrances in order to honour that word 'change', marked indelibly into their contract. Being constricted by a partner is quite simply a part of someone else's strategy, definitely not a feature of theirs. This gives the Air relationship an immediate advantage, for neither of these mercurial creations wants a relationship that falls short of interesting, stimulating conversation and a busy social life encompassing frequent changes of location. Perhaps unfairly so, Air has been accused of superficiality and an absence of human values in the sphere of human relationships. At the root of such behaviour lies the Air type's need to cover the widest range of experience possible. This need for intellectual intake and variety cannot be honoured by connecting with only one person. One man or woman alone is not capable of providing the miscellany of experience which Air seeks in life. Consequently, boredom often surfaces when they feel that a partner has dried up on them. Here we are considering a relationship between two similar types where, generally speaking, the cerebral takes precedence over the sexual, the intellect is raised above the emotions, and mind is superior to matter.

However, this does not bear the implication that Air types are uninterested in the more physical aspects of life. It means they simply lack depth. Air's initial forte is expansiveness, which accounts for a love of 'playing the field' when selecting a suitable partner. There are so many *interesting* people out there to discover. The Air type may be found displaying a marked talent for communication in the social world. Moreover, his adaptability allows him to relate to many different types of person from various walks of life. We can expect Air partners to embrace any new experience which may broaden their already unlimited horizons; certainly they would not consciously intend to limit the fields of each other. Indeed, as with other partnerships founded upon the same elemental type, their similarities allow for them to understand one another remarkably well. Hence Air partners appreciate each other's need for freedom and personal interests.

On another tack, Air is notorious for his fine, analytical mind, and his breezy knowledge of virtually every subject one could mention. His cleverness betrays him though, when he attempts to graft his logic on to the illogical world of human nature. He fails to apprehend the unpredictabilities and inconsistencies which go to make up the inner life of humans. Many Air people have a fixed catalogue of values regarding the behaviour of others. To him, certain things are just not *done*. This kind of intolerance makes its presence felt in niggling petty little ways, however reasonable an argument they may deliver. To highlight this, the individuals in an Air relationship often encounter their irrational other halves (symbolised by the Water element) in the external world with a critical, judgemental eye cast squarely on all those, 'bloody-minded neurotics' and 'sentimental mindless people who are just so unreasonable and illogical.' That is, the world of instinctive feeling must forever be condemned as emotional gush by the cerebral Air type.

And of course, messy emotions must *never* spill over into Air's romantic life, where the prevailing atmosphere is one of homogenised prettiness, elegance, refinement and good taste. Indeed, the polished manners of Air can often make those given to more ponderous and simple expressions feel slightly embarrassed and inadequate. Perhaps surprisingly, Air–Air bodes well for the marriage institution, even if closeness is somehow missing from the union. However, this can, and does, have its virtues. One of the conditions they make is that they should, perhaps above all, be friends besides being husband and wife.

Air Meets Water

As we have seen, one of the most common manifestations of male–female relationships results in the attraction of one's 'missing' half. In Air–Water combinations the polarisation seems to be particularly stressed. Water usually lacks the high-speed wit and cool-minded methodology of the Air type. On the other hand, Air is not blessed with Water's intuitive recognition of what lies beyond the surface of human beings. There is a definite fascination with those of the opposite sex who are the embodiment of our unconscious self, and who seem capable of handling the qualities we feel to be absent in ourselves. It is also common for partners to try and change each other; in this instance, Water would demand more sensitivity and a serious recognition of his feeling values, whilst at the same time forgetting that the flightiness of Air is his very attraction. Hence, were Water to succeed in this task, he would also, as a consequence, manage to dull the qualities which the partner happens to perform best. Air is likely to goad Water into being less emotional, and may even go so far as to berate him for the magnificent sin of showing feeling or releasing tears at an inopportune moment.

Air's quality of detachment is often an enigma to the Water person; Air may indeed possess the necessary qualifications to excel at everyday light conversation, the ability to direct his thinking habits, and a gift for dealing with people and making them feel welcome. It is these social skills in the market place of human affairs which Water finds magnetically attractive. However, what is not so palatable is to find oneself grappling with qualities in another than cannot fully come to expression in oneself. The conflict lies not between the individual and his partner, but within the individual himself. Water needs a partner with whom to share his wealth of feeling, and rarely evokes a genuine response from Air, who can seldom open himself up to another. As a consequence, Water does the emotional work for both of them. If Water cannot maintain a feeling of intimacy and closeness with a partner, he often becomes alienated and insecure and strains even more to elicit some kind of response – usually with emotional blackmail – while his inner self cries out to be loved. If the situation becomes as extreme as this, Air keeps a safe distance from that which he is barely able to comprehend in the first place.

Air's psychological orientation does not permit him an understanding of the feeling undercurrents invoked in an intimate relationship. Yet when unfamiliar emotions get the better of him they manage to wield more power than someone holding a shotgun to his head. This rupture in the orderly consciousness of the Air type manifests in disturbing, irrational moods. These threaten to erode the safe intellectual structure to which he often clings. Such an effect is experienced in this way because he is out of touch with his emotions. Consequently, Air often finds it particularly vexing in trying to relate to Water, who can, and usually does, emanate rather heavy emotional vibrations. These feelings, moreover, need not be verbalised for an airy partner to sense that the atmosphere has become stifled and claustrophobic with all kinds of unspoken resentment.

Many a Water person will atrophy a relationship in this way. If they feel hurt, they will refuse to discuss the matter, which, in turn, makes their moody silences positively unbearable. Fundamentally, Water is asking the Air type to hand over something which he does not possess, i.e. genuine depth and passion. It would, however, be more accurate to say 'cannot easily deal with'. In the Air type, emotions are still in their embryonic, unfashioned state.

Water Meets Water

When two individuals composed of the watery element come together, the net result may mirror that of the soul-searching trials of Cathy and Heathcliffe in *Wuthering Heights*. (A case study of these two lovers is presented in the following chapter.) By this I refer to the spiritual yearning for a soul mate, precipitating the archetypal Deeply Moving Experience – of which falling in love is one example of many – and when Water types fall in love, they do so with abandon. The principle characters in Brontë's tale of love obsession are, I think it safe to say, representative of the Water element. Such a type who has shared love with another and then separated will often cling tenaciously to the past which lives on in his interior wellsprings. One can thus imagine what happens when Water meets Water; each is at pains not to let go of the other, even in the most hopeless of situations.

The Water type who has inner security is a conducive partner for another of this element, blessed with the ability to make the partner feel especially loved and protected. This is not quite the same as Earth's responsible caring. Water's responsibilities lie in the area of human feeling, and thus will act as the guardian of another's emotions and sensitivities. Water is acutely aware of 'atmosphere' and two Water types will each possess a sixth-sense about how the other feels. It is this kind of psychic attunement which allows them to communicate on their own invisible, yet very intimate wavelength. Though Water may not articulate his perceptions well in a verbal sense, what he perceives in the world is often closer to the truth than he is given credit for. Water perceives the underlying realities of nature better than any other element.

However, intensity and profundity may bear the seed of another problem. Lack of polarisation between the partners can arise from the absent Air element. This 'missing' quality is often experienced in the surrounding environment with all of those 'cold intellectual types'. As Water is easily swayed by powerful emotion, one may witness the typical disagreements and irrational noise-making sessions (a distinct feature of a lack of Air). Yet no matter how this relationship might appear at the surface, Water types are unconsciously held together by an invisible thread that can withstand a considerable amount of strain.

Another kind of difficulty arises when partners of the same elemental type are too alike in temperament, and motivated by almost identical concerns. If it is true that we only become involved emotionally with those of the opposite sex who 'have something' for us, and that 'something' is the energy of our polar opposite, then partners of the same element may eventually cease to admire in the other that which they are easily capable of expressing themselves. Water is probably the least likely of the elements to embrace such an inner acknowledgement, simply because he cannot bear to give up a relationship. However, another Water person is the 'best' partner for the Water type, if only because they comprehend and appreciate each other's fathomless, unpredictable feeling nature.

Whereas the Earth–Earth alliance is driven by concerns about material stability, the Water types are ultimately seeking a kind of *emotional* stability. This is derived from having someone to care about who will also care about them. The security required by Water does not call for assured financial investments, a job in the high-earning bracket and a profuse supply of creature comforts, but reaches out for the kind of intangible support that is the consequence of intimate relationship with another. The partnership itself is enough to make each other feel safe. With this element the nurturing aspect works both ways. Water needs to care, and needs to be cared for. Certainly, they cannot bear to go it alone. Not ever.

CHAPTER 4

THE FATE OF RELATIONSHIPS

Burn will you please, my little one
Die so slowly
Caressed for so many years
You hung through those tears
A story of our time, the present moment plays
Of which you will find, something sinister to say
And it's time for a change, from this bestial fate
How I wish I could find, myself miles away.
Anon

Well to begin with, I don't envy *this* poor creature's fate in love; particularly with allusions to roasting embers, hellfire and damnation. Yet lost love and its accompanying tortuous emotions can evoke similar feelings; as if some vengeful demonic spirit has decided to punish us for getting our relationship all wrong, and we are somehow to blame. Such feelings of grey emptiness, particularly when stretched over a long period of time, move the individual to question whether or not he or she was cast into a relationship destined to fail.

There *is* an element of fate at work in our relationships, but scarcely with the individual acting only as a passive spectator. With hindsight, it will be seen that if we do not necessarily always get what we want, then we most certainly get what we need. I use the word 'need' to refer to what is required for the development of the psyche, thus, the self-awareness of the individual. A brief scan of the newspapers will testify to the fact that we are often quite ignorant of our inner selves.

Our handling of our relationships is far poorer than our advanced technological ideas. We fall for the new lover, become prone to the same unfulfilled expectations as before. Our new relationship takes on strikingly similar characteristics to the previous one. Ere long, the rift appears whereby we either become disillusioned and withdraw, or, even worse, our partner makes the sad announcement that, 'It's over.' Viewed from the periphery it certainly appears that many relationships are doomed to failure because 'something' continues to happen, eroding the foundations and threatening imminent collapse. The realisation dawns that we have become caught up yet again in another moribund affair. The rhetorical questions provoked in this not uncommon situation such as: 'When will the merry-go-round stop for me?' and, 'When will I find the *right* one?' are indications that the self has been excluded from the calculation. Rarely does one ask, 'What is it in me that attracts these painful situations?'

The recurring pattern running through many relationships whereby, 'He's just as demanding/tyrannical/neurotic as the previous one'; 'I've been through all of this before,' or, 'They have all tried to possess me,' tempts us to form the most rigid conclusions about the way men and women are. One only need eavesdrop on a conversation between two women who have suffered successive disappointments in their romantic lives, to see how such wrought-iron opinions as 'all men are selfish', effectively prevent the woman from taking note of her own shortcomings. This is hardly an exclusively female dilemma however, for males are prone to such similar unconscious assumptions which lead them to believe that females really *are* unintelligent, over sentimental, conniving, and submissive. When an individual meets again the same disenchanting experiences, the same emotional blackmailing games, and the same untimely rejections, and takes up with another lover only to discover he has fallen into the same fated web as before, he is witnessing the mark of that which he might least suspect – his unconscious mind. In making such observations one is acknowledging an inner process, an effect typical of the unconscious that wilfully asserts itself through conscious interaction with a partner. The relationship then assumes the function of a mirror, demonstrating how certain unconscious forces are behaving.

Psychology has much to say about these forces, which to ordinary ego consciousness appear mystifying, remote, hostile and otherworldly, but nevertheless filter through into the conscious life. They emanate from beyond the realm of memory and intuitions. They operate independently of the personal ego with which such forces are often in conflict. They drive the individual to behaviour which contradicts his best intentions. Various names have been coined for the living void out of which such unworldly experience arises: Universal or World Mind, Spirit Plane, Mind at Large, or the more scientific epithet, Collective Unconscious, the result of Jung's painstaking deductive enquiries.

Falling rapturously in love is just one manifestation of an impersonal energy working through the individual; impersonal since it pays no attention to our ego resistances and sweeps us along on a tide of feeling which mingles ecstasy with agony, hope with despair. If love's fatal aspects can in any way be laid upon the table of psychological scrutiny, then the area under consideration is to be the collective unconscious and its attendant archetypes, the irresistible forces of nature once considered to be gods. From the human standpoint they exhibit an awe-inspiring, omnipotent quality, capable of reflecting the ego at a fraction of its normal size. For example, consider the agents of irrevocable change which usher us on to the wheel of fortune with the call towards a particular vocation; the faculty which brings us to inner spiritual truths; the most intense and profound psychological transformations; and the frenzied depths of passionate love, all of which assume a power far greater than the ego's. These dynamic energies are built into the structure of nature. These are just some of the machinations of the archetypes.

Jungian psychology's terms for two of these archetypes are the feminine 'anima' (in males) and the masculine 'animus' (in females). But exactly what are these strange beings; what function do they perform? No one has ever seen an anima, though its effects are certainly met with in relationship. Moreover, it is unfortunate that most of Jung's own definitions for anima and animus lack a simplicity that may be conveyed to the layman. More often than not, they are described as images of the soul, or in Jungian analyst James Hillman's case, 'anatomy of personified notion'. This suggests that we are dealing here with abstract matters, the complex fragments of unresolved unconscious life. What it does not suggest is that these abstract matters are nonetheless very real indeed. The anima is whatever is feminine within the man, the animus masculine within the woman. Their subtle tamperings with the fate of an individual give them much to answer for, because their seductions of the ego lead it into the most fatalistic of relationships.

If a man were to describe all that he finds beautiful, mysterious and attractive in a woman then he would have illustrated the qualities of his own anima, the woman within. This is no phantasmagoria devoid of substance. He will have represented the sub-personality that is as much a part of him as his conscious ego. Thus, apart from the anima existing as an unconscious image of Ideal Woman and the begetter of expectations concerning actual females, she guides the inner psychological energies: feelings, impulses, moods and the like. Not only does the anima determine for him what women are like, it draws him to relationships with women who in some way resemble this inner figure, that is, females who consciously exude qualities found in the man's unconscious. Thus, to the male, women are like 'this' or 'that', not only due to his acquired experience of them, but because his experience of them depends on what he has attracted by virtue of his inner 'female' self.

The archetype who does our relating for us is summoned to 'life' in the manner of an animated character, when the anima and animus are given visible form in our love partners. Our hidden qualities are 'projected' on to the partner. This concept is not quite as abstruse as it first appears, for what *is* the world out there if not the qualities we project on to it? The qualities thus seen cannot arise without some participation of the psyche. Projection seems to be rather more than a clever philosophical idea of the way one subjectively views reality. The anima and animus appear to possess a definite substance, an energy, an emotional content.

Through the Taoist's eyes it is the masculine performed at the expense of the feminine, for where the yang is fully operative (e.g. in man), the yin must take expression elsewhere (in woman). The fine art of balancing must be learned therefore between conscious ego and unconscious anima, or man will project whatever he is 'lacking' (John Heider, *The Tao of Leadership*, Wildwood House, 1985):

> All behaviour consists of opposites or polarities. If I do anything more and more, over and over, its polarity will appear.

The anima will appear in projection; and if such energies behave according to their own guidelines, then it will be asked exactly what they are attempting to do. Arrive at conscious expression, the Jungian psychologist would answer.

These contrasexual personalities living beneath the surface of everyday consciousness are at the core of what we find breathtaking and seductive in others; without the magic, that first rush of romantic adrenalin, there could be no Special Someone in our lives. It is difficult for the conscious personality to accept that the dream lover is nothing more than an attractively spun web of illusion. The day dawns, however, when love dies, the relationship must come to an end or the partner leaves for someone else; this is the point at which the projection diminishes, perhaps love turns to indifference, and it becomes clear that the chimera within our brain has been deceiving us. Those visions of almost hallucinogenic loveliness, of our eternal heart's desire, were not inspired only by them, for our inner mind had reached out to include the object in its wellspring of fantasy. Yet, as I have stressed, projection is an entirely unconscious process, indeed as Jung points out, 'One doesn't make them, one *finds* them'. Thus we are permitted to believe that, in having 'found' attractive qualities in a lover, they will remain forever and continue to enchant. However, one is often made aware of a 'change' at some point in the process. This is where the initial rush of 'in-loveness' must, quite naturally, diminish somewhat, though this is far less painful than being jilted in love.

What Becomes of The Broken Hearted?

If the archetypes of relationship are our co-conspirators at the root of our 'fated' meetings with the opposite sex, and who apparently may enforce an eventual tragic separation, then what do they want from the mortal? The reason why we meet the love partner, and then believe we have found the 'right' one, has much to do with the elementary forces of attraction symbolised by the figures of the anima and animus. It is the unconscious in man and woman that pre-arranges many of the scenes they will witness during a love affair. One will always find in any apparently chance encounter with a potential lover, qualities existing within oneself – usually unconsciously. The anima carries with it the blueprint of what will come to pass in a man's relationship; perhaps this is why, when viewed from the ego's perspective, it holds such irresistible power and allure. The anima 'seduces' us into partnership many times over with people who wear the face of this inner archetype. We are always observing our own reflection.

This is easily understood when we have broken with a lover who in themselves resembles little the inner soul-figure. What attracted us to them in the first place were the creations of our own minds, the pictures thus hung upon them that, for a while, they were content to carry. In many cases where an individual has behind him a string of broken relationships, and he bravely attempts to 'try again', a kind of fate is establishing itself. It would be easy to conclude that such an individual has not yet found the 'right' one. One must look further and ask why these relationships never work out as expected; why they end with the same hurts and fragmented dreams 'filled with sadness and confusion'.

Perhaps it would be a good point of departure to enquire as to the reasons given by either partner for the break up – one partner too possessive; overbearing; lazy; wimpish; shallow. These are often subjective conflicts within the individual eventually projected upon the relationship, with considerable blame and bitter resentment. A former colleague of mine embodied a typical anima conflict in that he would fall violently in love with his 'latest', experiencing the raptures of heavenly bliss. Within a matter of weeks would come the news that they had 'finished' and he was back to square one having inherited considerable anguish and pain. The fate of this man's relationships seemed to rest positively in the hands of some greater unseen power. In these situations it is common perhaps to remark upon the individual's 'inability to hold down a relationship' or 'tendency to fall for the wrong ones'. Such analyses do nothing to shed light upon the inner situation. As with most valued life issues, the reality lies on the inside, and in this case the reality is the anima.

Whatever is 'missing' from conscious awareness gathers force in the unconscious. The general impression given by my friend would be as a rather solid, taciturn and deeply sensitive person, the qualities representing his conscious make-up. His anima, the unconscious silent partner, compensated by being fickle, shallow and impatient. That is, these qualities exist within *him*, but his anima becomes fickle and vain to the extent that the ego cannot, or will not, permit any such lightness to enter the conscious personality. His anima did not 'intentionally' attract women who would suddenly abandon him, nor was it intrinsically deceptive; it behaved the way it did because of his one-sided ego qualities of depth, compassion, sensitivity, profundity.

He was later able to maintain a steady relationship for several months and, ironically, was the one who did the leaving, with absolutely no remorse or regret. He had at last come to terms with part of his inner nature. By allowing some of the unconscious self to peep through, by permitting himself the occasional luxury of being 'light', superficial and unserious, he was able to release the anima into the conscious self. As for those sudden and upsetting departures* suffered at the mercy of previous women he had this to say: 'I was too heavy for them; it's no wonder they left me. I always *thought* I wanted a really serious relationship but as soon as I found one I backed out.'

Thus, as soon as the union he *thought* he wanted gathered momentum, his unconscious broke through. Instead of what usually happened (i.e. the partner leaving *him*), he became aware that his previous lovers' insistence on freedom and detachment, were a reflection of his own hitherto unrecognised demands for liberation. Hence, he always succeeded in gaining his freedom, though was simultaneously absolved of any responsibility in the matter – so his partner left him. In coming face to face with his own changeable and contradictory nature – primarily through relationships – and then living out the part himself, he was able to release the anima into its rightful vehicle of expression. When this is allowed to happen a transformation occurs in the psyche and the general tenor of one's relationships follow suit.

My friend does not incur the same hurts anymore. At the time of writing, his steady girlfriend of two years is expecting their baby with (he says) more to follow. It would be wrong to imply that the pain of the past has simply vanished

into thin air as though it never even
effects still linger on, though alongsi
wisdom. He has simply grown a new
Fitzgerald once wrote: 'A man does not r
jolts – he becomes a different person, and eve.
person finds new things to care about.' This is
become of the broken hearted.

Soul Mates

There exists a component of the psyche which engenders a
deep-seated longing for union, the meeting of 'souls' where
two persons become an indivisible one. Anyone who has not
felt the desire for that metaphorical closeness where the
presence of the other becomes as natural as one's own breath,
will simply not be able to appreciate the vastness of feeling
that one invokes in such a situation. The idea of the soul-
mate is so common a feature of relationships that it surely
warrants attention. Whether it is the immortal yearnings of
the soul for its rightful 'mate', or the fundamentally illusory
effects created by unconscious projection, this profoundly
moving experience, and its convincing power, is attested to
by countless people. It is the power that moves one to declare
only one true lover in one's lifetime, the love which even
death cannot end.

Esotericism proposes the existence of the spiritual 'mate'
in its explanation of the re-union of souls, a rendezvous
arranged by our higher selves, which may or may not occur
in this lifetime. Yet whereas psychology asserts that man is
potentially whole, the esoteric philosophy of soul-mates
maintains that he is incomplete and requires his spiritual
other half in order to fulfil his karmic destiny. Whilst there
remains the human tendency to fashion ideal images of the
opposite sex, and the stubborn feeling of uncanny familiarity
with the beloved in a love at first sight situation, it is the issue
of deep and passionate abiding love which concerns us now.
This drama from the abyss is such an intensely personal

that who is to say an individual is 'wrong' when ⟨de⟩clares emphatically that the woman who stands before ⟨h⟩im is his love, his life, his whole existence. Such seething emotions have, at times, proved to be dangerous, particularly in the light of lamentable suicide cases involving lovers. There are also instances where a widowed partner follows his beloved to the grave with such comparative suddenness, that one must conclude that he died of a broken heart.

Emily Brontë's sullen literary masterpiece *Wuthering Heights*, portrays the spectre of such pained love through its main protagonists, Catherine Earnshaw, and the latter-day Orpheus, Heathcliffe. It exemplifies perfectly the depths that are aroused through passionate love, and the manner in which they transcend the boundaries of a 'normal', 'healthy' relationship. In Cathy and Heathcliffe we witness the extraordinary bond of familiarity that is forged between lovers who know that they are each meant for the other. It is the kind of bond that geographical separation, family intervention, or even marriage to another partner cannot erase. It is not a matter of falling in love either, for the kind of love shared by Brontë's soul-mates (in the words of David Bowie) 'descends on those defenceless'. This suggests that a foreign species of emotion usurps the ego and renders it powerless to resist, despite its many attempts at remaining master of the house. Being hopelessly emotionally bound to another is a kind of fate. It is invoked without the sanction of the conscious mind, thus it acts as a kind of impersonal force which cannot be subordinated to the will of the individual.

Wuthering Heights evokes a startling vision of intense and profound love that descends upon the defenceless Cathy, the 'wild, sweet' headstrong girl from the rambling house on the Yorkshire moors; and the 'gipsy beggar' named simply Heathcliffe, of no fixed origin. He had been brought from Liverpool as a young boy to live at the Heights by Cathy's father. As time passes and the pair grow into young adults, Heathcliffe is forced to work as a stable hand (following the death of Earnshaw senior), while Cathy's brother Hindley assumes the mantle of master of the household. Cathy must adopt the role of the conforming younger sister. However, Hindley eventually falls prey to the degenerating effects of alcohol, proceeding to consume it in prodigious amounts that generate raging fits of drunken anger. Here is one character who plays a decisive role in the pact between the lovers, for his contempt for Heathcliffe and indifference towards Cathy serves to bring them closer together.

However, the lovers' fate becomes entangled when Cathy bows to what nineteenth-century society expected of a genteel young lady. It expected her to develop finesse and impeccable manners, study poetry, dress for dinner, and ultimately marry an honest, hard-working, respectable young man of similar tastes. This she found in Edgar Linton, a rather sententious though morally upright suitor. This drifting away from Heathcliffe into Linton's arms represents a familiar facet of female psychology. She opted for the security of middle-class family convention. In addition to its pretensions towards nobleness and superiority, this offered her wealth, stability and a safe passage through life. For this, Cathy was prepared to forego her love of Heathcliffe, yet at the same time acknowledged him as her soul ally: 'Whatever our souls are made of, his and mine are the same,' and carried one step further in the line to Ellen Dean: 'Nelly, I *am* Heathcliffe.' At which point a thunderbolt is heard loudly to pierce the rainy night sky, as if the gods were affirming her pronouncement as the divine truth. In spite of Cathy's inner acknowledgement, she and Linton are eventually married.

Here is where a theme in human nature arises. In resisting the inner archetypes with the superficial gloss of cultured intellect and all the excuses the ego can conceive of for disowning the most profound of emotions, the unconscious retaliates and makes its presence felt through other channels – the truth will out. Consequently, as Cathy is enclosed within the rosily secure walls of Thrushcross Grange, with attendant husband and sister-in-law, the ghost from her past, the soul-mate/animus, returns unbidden after a long absence to continue with the haunt. This is a metaphor for what happens when we attempt to rid ourselves of feelings we would rather not possess, when we try to mask the inner realities of Self; I will quote further from Daiche's introduction to the narrative: 'There is the recurrent and disturbing suggestion that the depths of man's nature are in some way alien to him.' Yet these depths are strangers only to the extent that we construct cast-iron ego qualities in order to banish them. We suffer the more for this estrangement when we meet our aliens in projection.

Heathcliffe returns metamorphosed from dishevelled stable boy into elegant, finely-honed gentleman with the social manners and possession of wealth to match. He has recently purchased Wuthering Heights, where he replaces the ailing Hindley as master. His close proximity to the Grange and Cathy, and his inevitable presence there, invokes a terrible conflict within the new Mrs Linton. It is exacerbated further when Heathcliffe eventually takes the Linton sister Isabella, for his wife. It is then only a matter of time before the inner situation reveals itself and Cathy's marriage to Linton is exposed as a convenient method of laying the ghost of Heathcliffe to rest. What follows poses the central question of whether or not soul unions actually occur. If certain relationships *are* pre-destined then something, somewhere is making the choices.

It is not the fact that Catherine Linton eventually perishes of a 'mysterious' illness (precipitated by Heathcliffe's marriage), or that Heathcliffe spews out so much vehement grief and bitterness at witnessing his 'love and life' so perilously close to death, which begs the question of fated love. It is that the lovers were somehow destined to come together, never to be separated. Firstly, one learns of the boy Heathcliffe introduced into the family by Earnshaw senior. From the young Catherine's point of view, this represents a kind of fate imposed by the family circle, something she could only choose to avoid when she had grown up, or by having run away from home there and then. As we have seen, she elects to do the former. She grows up with him participating in the same childhood pleasures, tears and passions, until she realises that he has grown to be the guardian of her soul. Despite her uncontrollable love for him, she chooses to marry into a prosperous family unit, and if this story were being told today about a real-life pair of lovers, it would most likely end there. However, such forces as these are anything but 'civilised'. Eros chooses to live through the mortal regardless of personal choice or volition, and as such represents a fate still encountered by numerous individuals today. The gods are immortal. The fate invoked by Cathy, intimately linked to her obsessive and poisonous love for Heathcliffe, is one in which the ego has virtually no power to resist. As befits all good tragedies, she must eventually die of a broken heart.

'Be with me always – take any form – drive me mad – only do not leave me in this abyss where I cannot find you. I cannot live without my life... my soul.' These are the words spoken by Heathcliffe to the dead Catherine. Such utterances cut straight to the heart, stripping away the need for any intellectual discourse on the nature of passionate love – but was she really his 'soul'? One could speak on either of two levels here: either the protagonists were destined to meet on the physical plane due to prior arrangement by their 'higher selves'; or their respective inner relating archetypes, the anima and animus, were directing most of the action via unconscious projection. In *How To Find Your True Soul Mate*, James F. Cullinan is unequivocal on the subject of the spiritual mate: 'Accept right now that your soul-mate exists . . . a person in a sea of bleak soulic-loneliness who is longing for a soulic-unification with you!' Amen.

Psychology's discovery of the soul partners, though not quite soul *mates*, brings these lofty suppositions down to earth. Even if the anima and animus are not exactly creatures of the material plane, their fundamental effects are demonstrable in that they impinge upon the fate of an individual's relationship. They differ from the spiritual soul-mate in that the archetypes may be realised as part of the unconscious psyche and thus worked with, experienced and partially integrated into conscious life. In contrast, concerning soul-mates, one is apparently given little choice in the matter. I am inclined to ask, as Jung might have done himself, what would have been the outcome if Heathcliffe had realised that Cathy was the incarnate version of his own anima and had sought to understand the nature of his own projections?

If the anima and animus constitute part of our own inner natures, then we ourselves actively participate in the unfolding fate of our love lives. Working with these archetypes helps to dispel some of the fatalistic overtones of relationships. Even in having made such an effort, anima and animus will continue to assert themselves in perhaps subtler fashions. Certainly, their influence is felt to varying degrees of intensity in every male–female relationship under the sun. One's innate desire to love may not create such tragic repercussions as those of Brontë's fictional characters, yet even the best of us are driven by unconscious demands and expectations often with an unvoiced, you-must-respond-to-me clause. The stubborn, underlying assumption that the partner ought consistently to react and behave towards us in a certain manner is the silent note sounded by the inner figures. The image fashioned in the unconscious, when not understood, exerts its demands for expression through the least line of resistance. That so often means the partner.

It would be easy to maintain a happy partnership if one could accept the partner entirely on their own terms. Unfortunately, this is rarely the case, and thus many disappointments precipitate between partners. Indeed, we often feel let down. Relationships are rooted so deep in emotion that the advice to 'accept your lover as they are' proves exceedingly difficult to carry out in practice. One must consider the inner demands of the contrasexual, unconscious archetype. For instance, the relationship may proceed smoothly as long as the partner, intuitively responding to our signal, continues to respond as we should wish, 'carrying the projection'. However, our unconscious wears the face of resentment when our partner fails to react as we would like. The ensuing ambience resembles that of the over sensitive and moody child where one 'wrong' word is taken directly to the heart. Then the reaction becomes swollen out of all proportion. This intrusion of obstinate feeling that the anima and animus perpetrate must be honestly evaluated if we are to function as conscious beings in our relationships. If we continue to hold on to that wonderful image of the lover, we shall see many of our expectations die a premature death and perhaps withdraw into the conclusion that we have chosen the wrong one, whilst the anima and animus have been instrumental in the 'choosing' all along.

One is able to discern the difference between projected image and corporeal partner when, for one reason or another, love dies for us and we become intensely dissatisfied with our present relationship. What a revelation it comes, to discover that we didn't really love the monster/iceberg/bully/prima donna after all, hot on the heels of an inner realisation that little 'me' in here *also* has individual desires and opinions. This is a typical female pattern, whereby the woman falls in love and gets married, settles into domesticity and after several years (or perhaps only months) realises that she deserves better. She chafes against her situation as the animus takes up abode in her consciousness. It is not only women who succumb readily to the will of a partner, a phenomenon made clear by the stereotyped nagging old battle-axe whose husband is the self-effacing, physically slight, hen-pecked wimp, an image so beloved of the seaside picture post-card industry. Many of our love affairs, it transpires, turn sour through lack of practice as an individual; the fear of asserting one's personal desires, independence, ambitions, and dare I say, *selfishness*. Even within a relationship there is something in human beings that respects a certain amount of autonomy or 'separateness' in others. In fact, it is found to be attractive. Whether it is lauded as being one's own man or woman or chastised as plain selfishness, the 'self-made' individual is somehow alluring. Are *they* less fated in relationships?

The answer to that question is most likely 'no', for each of us must carry an imprint of the relating archetype whose needs must be met. However, as we allow more of the inner figure to be realised, having first apprehended it in others, we open the door to a greater awareness of Self and environment, and the psychological interaction between the two. This is the point at which Eros is recognised as a component of the individual psyche. Thus, it is we who are mostly responsible for the fated patterns in our relationships, though that responsibility hinges also upon the activities of the inner mind and what is 'down there'. What is down there can only be worked with and transformed through relationship with others if we are to come to terms with any painful, fatalistic demons in the unconscious. We must continue with the search instead of retreating into brooding loneliness. Only that way will they be released and their power diminished. As befits the paradoxes of life, we must first succumb to our fates in order to be free of them. Unless of course, like James F. Cullinan, you know better.

CHAPTER 5

LOVE OBJECTS
A WARNING

By falling in love we participate, as Proust puts it, 'in a play not with a woman of the external world, but with a doll fashioned in our brain'. William Faulkner was just as insightful on this matter: 'The ideal woman which is in every man's mind is evoked by a word or a phrase, or the shape of her wrist, her hand. Every man has a different idea of what is beautiful, and it is best to take the gesture, the shadow of the branch and let the mind create the tree.' A man's anima shapes fantasies around an actual woman when the woman expresses herself in ways which conform to the inner figure. Letting the 'mind create the tree' may be fine for painters and songwriters, but it proves extremely problematic, not to say painful, when one fails to interpret the difference between the inner archetype and the person who stands before you.

The early Greek writers seemed to 'know' all about unconscious projection; in the myth of Pygmalion (from Ovid's *Metamorphoses*) the central figure projects his anima on to an ivory statue which is the embodiment of his own, idealised woman. Pygmalion was a king with such exacting standards of feminine perfection that no one mortal woman could ever equal them. So he carved out a beautiful lifelike statue in order to give shape to this image, which he christened Galatea. He would pass many hours gazing in rapture at this marvellous example of womanhood. It seemed so real that he would gingerly touch it to reassure himself that it was in fact only a sculpture. Normally, this act would have offended

Aphrodite, the patroness of physical beauty and presider over matters of love. The offence of *hubris* came from lack of humbleness before the divine, and Galatea was possessed of a radiance on a par with that of the goddess herself. Instead of being insulted by Pygmalion's handywork, the goddess took pity on him and brought the statue to life so that he might experience his ideal woman in the flesh. Thus ends a poignant allegory of psychological projection – the feminine uniting principle (symbolised by Aphrodite) brings the soul figure to 'life' in a corresponding actual female. Like Pygmalion, the male may never suspect that his love object, overflowing with bejewelled enchantment, is a reflection from the world within.

The myth of Pygmalion illustrates the extent to which all of us live in a subjective world. One finds parallel examples in Hugo's *Quasimodo* and *Esmerelda*, Leroux' *Phantom of The Opera*, and a more recent illustration of the phenomenon in Danny Kaye's portrayal of Professor Frisbee in the 1948 film, *A Song Is Born*. What united these characters is (in direct contrast to their unprepossessing appearance) that they fell in love with a beautiful object, and one may be forgiven for taking the situation to mean no more than that. In doing so, they unmasked the beauty that lay *within* them, the intangible soul figure, and re-created its likeness in a corresponding external object. Of course, one could argue that the object possesses attractive properties of its own and that in itself constitutes its drawing power. One must also ask whether we can, in fact, ever truly observe the world out there as it exists in itself. The more one tries to assert, for instance, that a woman possesses glamorous and radiant qualities of her own, i.e. is beautiful in herself, the more one must remember that the world derives its qualities only from one's inner, psychological content. Or as Milton puts it, 'What thou seest, what thou there seest, fair creature, is thyself.'

The beholding eye that is blind to all else surfaces at all levels of experience. The time-honoured 'what does she see in him?' (reverse genders if you wish) attests to something within the individual beholding eye that quite obviously does not appear to others. It matters less to the one thus infatuated what the object's 'actual' traits are, than the image built around it. It would be fine if we could all live in a constant, unspoiled nirvana, laced with the appropriate romantic illusions, if only the world of cold reality would not press its face up against our window. For example, the young princess (in reality, a chip shop assistant) does not wish to know any of the hard facts about her handsome prince (in reality, a bricklayer's apprentice with acne). Wake up fair princess, wake up, I say.

Men also project their internal dreams upon flesh and blood females. Even when no woman is present in their lives they are often besieged with a powerful emotion which stirs up a kind of stubborn resolution which says, 'This woman exists somewhere out there and I've got to find her.' The ego is so utterly convinced that these myriad qualities are to be found waiting in an actual woman, that one must assume the unconscious produces some extremely potent and compelling forces. The anima contains something awe inspiring, something exotic. The figure fashioned in one's brain does indeed take on human form via projection, yet the ego is so overwhelmed that it cannot differentiate between inner image and corporeal woman. This phenomenon is suitably illustrated in John Fowles' vision of Victorian England, *The French Lieutenant's Woman*, a portrayal of the unworldly power of the anima set against the conventional mores of Lyme Regis in the nineteenth century. It depicts one man's discovery of the absurdity of the heart, even though he himself is the kind of fellow we are to assume is beyond all such caprice. Charles Smithson is a level-headed gentleman–scientist of his day, much given to upholding the moralistic traditions of Victorian society. He lays claim to a thoroughly rational and pragmatic approach to problem solving. He considers himself intellectually superior (a Darwinian) to most others of his kind, yet these gifts prove to be worthless when facing his nemesis – the conjuror in his soul, his anima.

The young man is about to take the hand in marriage of Ernestina Freeman, a typical product of the female of the late nineteenth century. Then it was assumed that being dressed in excessive apparel and sporting a virtually white complexion were the supreme examples of feminine propriety. However, it is whilst in Lyme Regis that Smithson encounters 'Tragedy', a woman of somewhat dubious reputation who gazes out to sea awaiting the return of a man she had chance to encounter in most unfortunate circumstances. There are two phrases I have used in the foregoing sentences – 'dubious reputation' and 'unfortunate circumstances' – which allude precisely to the kind of language one might encounter in that hypocritical Victorian era. They reflect the theme of Fowles' novel (and to an extent this book). The passions of the human heart are too easily frowned upon by less perceptive though so-called authoritative figures. In taking society's condemnations to heart, too seriously, the 'guilty' person is landed with the dichotomy of that which he ultimately longs for and desires, and the perfunctory role he must play because of societal expectations. Hence, Smithson, the gentleman scientist, must ostensibly live up to the rigorous standards set by the epoch he finds himself in (though this pressure applies equally today), by his peers, his profession, and his involvement with Ernestina, that monument to prim, saccharine respectability. However, all of that is soon to change.

It is often the man of words, developed intellect and superior rationality, who falls unwittingly for the emotional and changeable-as-the-wind female, the kind of woman through whom he is apt to discover that 'all women are unreliable, illogical, gushing and unstable'. These are the negative attributes of his own anima, fashioned on the reverse side of his logical and laudable virtues. It is ultimately to this emotional and insightful woman, who instantly comprehends the logic of the heart, that his soul belongs. It is here where Smithson draws the unavoidable comparison between the 'scarlet woman of Lyme', Sarah

Woodruff, and the lady Freeman. These qualities belong to Miss Woodruff, and it is during Charles' encounter with her in a secluded wood that he apprehends being overcome and held virtually captive by an unfamiliar feeling. The numinous power of the anima often completely erodes away the feeble resistances of the ego. Smithson (in Fowles' own words) '. . . felt outwitted . . . the forbidden was about to engage in him . . . it was as if, when she was before him, he had become blind.'

It is with so many misgivings that Charles must eventually concede defeat to the enchantress in his soul and its projection onto the enigmatic Miss Woodruff. His cherished sense of realism is thrown into disarray as he realises he is falling in love with her. As befits the Honourable Gentleman, Smithson is obliged to break off his engagement to the worldly Ernestina, and as an unfortunate side-effect, must become the object of scorn to many of his fellow men, a figure of hate to his erstwhile, prospective father-in-law. He is to become a social outcast for committing the crime of falling in love with the French Lieutenant's Woman. However, before he will fully acknowledge it in himself, he must assume the mask of the helpful samaritan, the goodly citizen, and aid the unfortunate Miss Woodruff in getting away from Lyme and her existence as an outcast. With each and every encounter with her, Charles's anima is powerfully evoked. Later on, the inevitable intimate encounter transpires. By then the madness has sufficiently caught hold, and thus he dutifully returns to Lyme to disband his marriage plans to Ernestina.

It is in Fowles' ultimate conclusion to the story that we discover so much that is concealed behind Smithson's coldly conventional exterior. It is almost inconceivable that such a rational man should waste many months in search of a mystery woman who invites only an uncomfortable emotion. In Fowles' second and true 'ending', Charles returns from Lyme to the place where Sarah has hitherto been ensconced, only to find that she has disappeared. Thus begins the long and painful search. It is after a period of two agonising years that he at last finds her, only to be met with cruel indifference, and a transparency which forces him to see that there is no one at home to Charles Smithson. Sarah's forgiveness towards his passions in the heat of this moment is most telling in Charles' anima. He had elicited some of the real Miss Woodruff, the one no longer carrying the projection; her oblivion to his pain, makes him (according to Fowles) ' . . . the victim of a conquest of irrational law over rational intent.'

In becoming the victim of such an irrational law, that is the ensnarement of love, he was soon to learn that to play with fire requires protective clothing. He exited from their final meeting with his fingers badly burned. Sarah had outgrown him and 'found' herself. Their initial meetings were founded upon (for her) much ambiguity towards how she truly felt about Charles. She had never said, for instance, 'Let us steal away together somewhere and be married and live happily,' though that is how Charles had interpreted the situation. Owing to the engulfing emotions of the anima, he took this interpretation as a precept for all his subsequent actions – the two-year long impassioned quest to find her.

Projection onto the unattainable lover is a typical motif among writers. A similar theme as Fowles' arises in Thomas Hardy's *The Well Beloved*, in which the central character, Pierston, pursues and loves three women from separate generations of the same family: the first beloved, her daughter, and her granddaughter. He is pursuing the ideal embodiment of his inner woman. In the words of an introduction to Hardy's novel, this figure is 'really his own self image, his wraith or double in a changed sex.'

To return to Fowles, one could in retrospect argue that Charles Smithson was simply an incurable romantic unable to deal with his powerful infatuation, until one remembers that this man neither expresses tendencies towards romanticism, nor exhibits traits normally associated with someone who would develop an obsessive emotional attachment. He is ostensibly a man of science, objectivity and the rational world, and conducts his life in accordance with that basic outlook. It is only when he is caught unawares by an under-current of intense feeling, possessed by inimical disturbing passions, that we see the underside of Mr Smithson's psyche. These qualities exist within him, and wherever *we* go in the world *we* discover our inner selves looking back at us.

The icon of feminine allure embodied in Sarah Woodruff need not be met on stormy stone piers or in secluded woodlands in such idyllic places as Dorset. She is a facet of the feminine whose face is worn by women every day and everywhere. She is neither loud nor talkative and does not overtly try to draw attention to herself. If she is pretty then so much the better. It reinforces the value of her outer, delicate sheen – poised, 'sweet', retiring. Certain men want to dis-cover her inner secrets and try to get her to reveal herself, apprehending so much that is concealed behind the veil. Yet men lured by this anima figure often receive a rude awaken-ing when they discover that the actual woman possesses an obstinacy, an argumentativeness and an immovability. When the woman conspicuously embodies such traits, she has become a guest of the animus.

The Hidden Logos – The Animus

The animus in woman is, as we might expect, met with in the ideal of her lover, husband, brother, father, etc. The father is one of the shaping influences in the role that the animus will play in the life of a woman, just as the mother colours the male's anima with whatever emotional atmosphere was cre-ated in his childhood. Like any archetype it may assume a variety of different guises, but will always reflect the man (both inner and outer) with whom she is required con-sciously to come to terms. The animus most likely presents a greater difficulty for women than does the anima for males. Whereas men may admit to their inner softness and need to relate emotionally, societal roles embody certain problems if the woman is to realise fully and bring into play, the impersonal, isolated sense of selfhood that is represented by this archetype. The animus is a spirit of de-personalised logic, the masculine voice which tells her that she is an individual being, and not someone's mother, lover, mistress, daughter, or fantasy object. It attempts to assert itself in her, and the sooner she realises what it is, the better.

As with the male's inner woman, a female's animus usually acquires its degree of power in relative proportion to any one-sided ego qualities. The image of Perfect Man residing in her unconscious appears in stark contrast to the woman's own self image – where she may be physically slight, timid and self-effacing, her animus may appear as the robust warrior, brimming with charismatic self-confidence; where a woman may be extroverted, freedom-loving and 'happy go lucky', she may be fettered to an unconscious ideal of the conservative, scholarly and inward-looking man. The animus and anima archetypes acquire such a magical hold over the ego precisely because of their remoteness from the qualities contained in consciousness. The notion or image is furnished with fascinating and attractive properties because they are underdeveloped and unlived. The result is the mutual attraction of opposites. The more these attributes are made known in oneself, the less do they stand in opposition to the ego personality, for the opposite is oneself also.

The inner relating archetypes engender stubborn convictions regarding the opposite sex. Whereas the negative face of the anima produces irrational feeling and emotional effects, the animus imparts to the woman dogmatic assumptions usually borrowed from the market place of collective opinion. Giving voice to such logic is not an intrinsic quality of the man within woman. It is a clouding of the true nature of the animus, for he symbolises the *Logos* principle, the spirit of clear reflective judgement and the capacity for independent thought and action. Whereas these qualities may be expressed in their truest form in males (a generalisation, I hasten to add), they arise in a modified version in the female psyche when her opinions are tainted with emotional experience. To exemplify the workings of a negative animus, there is the world of difference between true objective thought and the expressing of opinions which bear an unmistakable second-hand quality where 'everyone knows that . . .', and 'men are always so . . .'. It is in the latter case where the animus is standing behind the woman's expressions, so often dictated in this way because of a negative experience of men.

Disappointments with the love object point to something unconscious – the animus – attempting to work itself out. Whereas the male's anima is coercing him to relate on a feeling level and to straddle the boundaries which exist between man and woman, the animus urges the woman to stand alone and appreciate the true spirit of impersonality. It is a matter of balance. The more vociferous and independent female who shuns involvement in a relationship, whose intention it is to become politically active, or who smokes a pipe at the company board meeting, may be quite unaware that the individuality she values may be an unconscious stab in the back to her own femininity. Her ability to make her own choices, pursue her ambitions and debate ecological issues at protest rallies, may be a concealed reaction to her own inability to relate in a feminine way. However, in the majority of cases it is expressed in projection. The animus infuses the love object with the masculine qualities which belong to the woman's unconscious. Another case example may help to illustrate the phenomenon.

For this account, I would like to return to the example cited earlier of the 'physically slight, timid and self-effacing' female, whose Ideal Man is the 'robust warrior, brimming with charismatic self-confidence'. The following events demonstrate how qualities absent from consciousness can retain such a hold over an individual when animated in a person of the opposite sex. Psychologically speaking, the charismatic and robust warrior is a facet of the shy coquette herself. How is the woman to acknowledge this? My friend, whom I shall call Anna, resembles the type of young woman one might find gracing the covers of a magazine advertising matrimonial wear, with its attendant romantic images. She is what one might describe as a conventionally pretty, petite and 'feminine' female. Part of her psyche is arrested by the image of the 'hunky', vigorous and domineering kind of male. Eventually, this is what she found in Robin, the embodiment of all her ideals. Their liaison lasted no longer than four months since Robin was about to begin a two-year college stint in another part of the country, and (according to him) travel would prove exceedingly difficult. In any case, he soon became involved with other girls at the college as he had formed no deep emotional ties to Anna. But for her there *was* no one else, or more appropriately, no one else around who exhibited the kind of qualities she experienced as perfect examples of masculinity.

After a period of several months Anna flitted briefly in and out of relationships, to relieve the upset of finding herself alone again. None of the males she experienced had any lasting effect on her since the only man she could intimately connect with was one like Robin. By being bound to such a personification of her unconscious she left Robin with the key to unlock her heart, a man who is neither attractive, well-mannered or particularly engaging for that matter. Anna was blind to any of this, for what mattered was what brought her inner figure to life. She saw in him the living embodiment of her idea of the Perfect Man, even though others would not call to mind an adjective such as 'perfect' on meeting him.

On the surface, Anna's stubborn infatuation with such a male appears to display an act of deliberate perversity – how *could* such an attractive and amiable girl fall for such a dislikeable fellow? The answer lies not in any conscious intention, or to rebel against her parents, but in the conflict between her outer feminine self and the stranger within. It is this stranger dwelling within the depths of Anna's unconscious which prevented any real relationship with the men she met after her affair with Robin. As these men came and went, Anna's memory would immediately return to the ideal she had discovered and lost. She would find herself murmuring, 'If only I could find someone like Robin'. She is still waiting for him.

Were Anna to discover her own capacity for dynamic, ardent self-promotion – essentially to express her inner masculinity – then her animus would occasionally find its way out from behind the glossy skin of her feminine expressions. But as the image of herself as the complete embodiment of womanly charms forbids this, she is still waiting for him. Nevertheless, the animus will find its own ways of visiting her.

We will now look to another example to illustrate the functioning of the inner man, an example set in almost direct contrast to our 'coquette' whom we might reasonably call the 'lively tomboy'. Our effervescent and 'boyish' female – whom I shall call Julie – was caught up in a succession of disappointing affairs, often at the bidding of her animus. It requested in its own silent yet forceful manner, the recognition not of her inner self-assertive masculinity, but of her need to play down such masculine characteristics. That is, the masculine was well in evidence in her outer personality. By virtue of this, an imbalance was created in her psyche because her natural and instinctive feminine qualities were continually overshadowed. She experienced an anima problem too – the difficulty with embodying so called feminine traits.

The need to harmonise and soften her outer persona was made plain in the number of men who were subsequently rudely awakened by Julie's assertive and dynamic qualities; qualities which they expected only to find in their drinking partners at the local pub. Yet there was something refreshingly alive about this girl. The men with whom she formed relationships were initially attracted by her buoyant spirits, her candour and generosity, her warm friendly exterior, and the effortless ease with which she could deflate the most pompous and stuffy people. In spite of her gregarious sociability, one could often detect a hint of sadness behind her smiling eyes, the inner wound beyond the hail-woman-well-met facade.

Julie experienced her first 'great love affair' with Alex around the age of twenty three. It was so pleasing to her that as soon as it suddenly atrophied, Julie was plunged into a long period of emotional pain. She lived then with confusion, depression and a keenly felt emptiness about the whole of her life. This experience was the first major emotional wound she had suffered, the initial cutting of the heart in two, which is ultimately the catalyst for awareness. The dawning of wisdom is often illuminated by pain. It was the element of the tomboy, advertising a lack of feminine softness and subtlety, which brought about the final split. Her boyfriend quite simply wanted her to be more 'womanly', being unable to endure her outspokenness. It would be another long three years before she would truly love again, before she could find within her the capacity to open herself emotionally to another again.

Before her next major relationship she had met with several men and experienced various brief liaisons. None of these was satisfying or long lasting. With hindsight, these short affairs were important since they depicted the animus at work. Two particular brief encounters exemplify what was attempting to come to light within her, two relationships which also confirmed to Julie that she was never meant to have a lasting love affair. The first of these, with Paul, was a rather one-sided affair, Paul playing the role of the receptive, loving and attentive partner. Julie could never quite bring herself to reciprocate his affections. Outwardly, she went along with the charade, like so many Hollywood starlets posing happily for the camera, whilst shielding a heartache which seems unwilling to go away. Eventually she bade her farewells to the kind and responsive Paul, causing him much hurt and resentment in the process.

Her second encounter, with John, could hardly even have been called a relationship, based as it was on so many broken dates, uncertainty, lack of direction and John's annoying tendency to keep as much distance as possible. Beyond this futile game the animus was at work. She had recently begun to discover the capacity to love again. Slowly but surely, the dim heartache was dying away.

We can gain much information about the qualities of the animus and the function it was seeking to fulfil by looking at the kind of qualities Julie initially found attractive in the three men cited above, and the eventual consequences she experienced. The animus invariably derives its nature from the unlived out content of the psyche, compensating for the energies recognised and expressed by the ego. In Julie's case, this resulted in her attracting men who embodied qualities of gentleness, subtlety, reflectiveness, deep feeling, and who exuded a rather conservative personality. Indeed, despite her often unconventional and sloppily attired persona, Julie is fond of the 'business suit': clean cut, short hair, tidily dressed. Her outward face, that of the happy-go-lucky adventurer, the gregarious free spirit, looks outward to see the face of the unconscious: the man of profound depth, serious reflection, practical wisdom, possessing the key to the problems of the mundane world, qualities she found in both Alex and Paul. Such qualities were projected upon these two men as a result of her need to come to terms with them in herself.

Her suitors felt threatened by her open-mannered friendliness with other male acquaintances, being unprepared to share her company and attention with anyone else. Many times over there would be complaints from her partner about the kind of social circles in which she moved. They would have been gratified had she had no other male acquaintances. As this began to pose serious problems, she ended the relationship with Paul because of his 'jealous streak'. One must look beyond the superficial reasons given in such a situation: the animus was trying to tell her something. Consciously she was well acquainted with herself as the bright and lively-minded optimist, the joyful freedom lover. She was unable to recognise that aspect of herself which sought to establish deep connections, roots and the containment of life. This she projected on to her male partners, and saw its negative facets of jealousy and possessiveness, or the more instinctive and earthier elements of relating. Inwardly, Julie herself contained elements of possessiveness. In its basic form this is the need to establish a strong feeling bond with something, to hold on to it and make it part of oneself. Since she had little inkling of her capacity for forming strong ties, she met with this rather heavy-handed and intensely jealous aspect of human nature in her male lovers/friends. The man within was scolding her for refusing to acknowledge her own inner depths, confronting her with the shadowy attributes of her own psyche. This darkness her carefree exterior could barely begin to betray.

After several months of self-evaluation, Julie felt ready to enter into a relationship proper. That she discovered intense passion, earthiness and a dark brooding quality in her next partner ought to come as no surprise – the natural pull of the animus. Since she was now prepared to operate on a feeling level the relationship fared much better than her previous encounters. She discovered that for the second time in her life she had fallen in love. Though being inwardly afraid of rejection, she made the effort at a true partnership, now prepared to give herself in a way she had not done since her affair with Alex. The unconscious had propelled her into a union which reflected the energies of her undiscovered self.

After several months, she was forced again into a confrontation with the beast within. What permitted this relationship to endure for so long was that her new partner had allowed her greater freedom than in her previous experience, and had tolerated some of her more exuberant and excessive tendencies. The relationship died because she could no longer endure the powerful moods and eventual exasperation of a partner who balked at her entertaining noisy house guests until 4 a.m. in the morning.

In retrospect we can see a thread, a quality pervading the whole of Julie's relationships: her experience of the shadowy, unprepossessing figure within, an image which apparently wanted to bind her restless soul in chains and 'possess' her. What did the animus really want? It required a recognition of her powerful inner drives, 'bad' emotions and compulsions. She used these successfully to evade responsibility by living in the safe world of surface attractions. She was unwilling to risk the confrontation with all that was dark and shadowy within herself, and had she permitted the emergence of natural though raw emotions into her relationships – those which would connect her to the realm of subterranean feeling – she would have experienced less conflict. She would have been able to bridge the gap between what she could only see as her partner's jealousy and her own happy-go-lucky self.

Classic fiction provides identifiable models through which one may glean the workings of the relating archetypes; an example to compare with that of John Fowles' novel is D.H. Lawrence's short story, *The Virgin And The Gypsy*, a forerunner of the infamous *Lady Chatterley's Lover*. Here, Lawrence sets his heroine, Yvette, against a backdrop of clerical life in a pious household peopled by her vicar father, her aunt and uncle, and an obnoxious hard-of-hearing grandmother. Yvette's only true companion was her sister, Lucille.

The animus often acquires its own properties in contrast to the self-image, thus the ostensibly prim and virtuous Yvette, the product of a sanctimonious vicarage cleansed of all primary instincts, develops an awareness of the ghostly lover, her inner animus. This gipsy-soul within develops its power in proportion to her chaste, conventional background reflected in family life at the vicarage.

The animus archetype is timeless and amoral, beyond the call of the conventions of any period of history. It is that pre-existent maleness awaiting consciousness in the woman, and consequently ushering her towards a true relationship with the world of the masculine principle, wherever it may be found. However, as the animus (like the anima) is not an inherent property of the *individual* unconscious (i.e. it is transpersonal), it also inspires mystery. It evokes subtle yet immensely fascinating images, poetic almost divinely inspired longings for the love object. 'If only some magical being would come and rescue me,' says the woman moved by the animus.

And so the rural gypsy becomes a focus of distraction for Yvette; his nomadic, primitive aura is somehow enchanting to her, despite his lack of refinement, manners and the usual perfunctory social gestures. He exhibits a kind of charismatic animal grace, the kind of instinctive stealth which a tiger might display whilst eyeing its prey, and where one is simultaneously in awe of both its beauty and malign deadliness. The fact that he may be nothing more than a simple rough-and-ready wanderer is of little consequence. The sensuous and captivating gypsy is what lives inside her, and like Charles Smithson she attempts to fend off the enchantment by force of reason. In the object she perceives mystery, the darkness which beckons, and the portal to the nether worlds. He invokes in her a dream, 'which she could not shake off'. The inner figures assume some independent life of their own and a game ensues between the rationalising ego and the unconscious. Lawrence writes: '"No, he hasn't any power over me," she said to herself, rather disappointed really, because she wanted somebody, or someone to have power over her.' In other words, she had acknowledged some unconscious force beginning to assert itself, especially in reaction to the coquettish and crinolined, mostly pampered child that was Yvette. Thus before long, her imagination submits to the compelling fantasies about her gypsy 'lover', fired by her close proximity to the camp where his family have temporarily come to rest. Her attention is caught by the rustic and simple existence of these gypsies; the open fire, dirty children playing nearby, horses roaming freely. It is this image of unfettered rural tranquillity which evokes the 'gypsy' within her. Inevitably she thus attracts his attentions. It is beneath her to make advances towards *him*, not because he is a simple gypsy, but because of her social position.

The climax to Lawrence's short story is reminiscent of the

Hades/Persephone myth from classical Greece; both contain elements of natural disaster, a shadowy intruding figure, and the initiation of a young maiden into womanhood. The elemental gypsy and Hades-Pluto are both animus figures rising from the female's (Yvette-Persephone) unconscious to herald the encounter with hitherto undiscovered masculine energies. Even if the gypsy is not quite the rapist that was the god of the underworld, the girl Yvette's initiation ceremony, like that of Persephone's, is precipitated by a freak catastrophe, a dynamic natural force as irrevocable as thunder and lightning. The eruptions of the unconscious are thus portrayed in symbols as new life breaks through and the psyche admits the realities of the animus.

The grand entrance of this incontrovertible masculine force is depicted in Lawrence's story as a mighty swell of water threatening to engulf the house as the nearby river suddenly and violently begins to overflow. This virtual desolation by the overflowing river symbolises the stripping away of the false values of the ego (represented by the house) by the natural forces of instinct which flow unpredictably beneath it. Her psyche can thus no longer admit the suffocating holiness and piety of this environment. The unconscious bursts forth to offer a glimpse of her unknown inner self. Poignantly, the flood does not destroy her, but the structure with which she has become identified. Her neglected unconscious erupts not to destroy her ego (i.e. drive her insane), but to lay waste the pretensions inimical to her true, inner self. At this crucial point, most appropriately, the gypsy appears, as if he and the natural cataclysm are the same thing. He then takes hold of her arm as they both find themselves struggling through the garden, now transformed into a river, stumbling almost blindly through the rising water, along the path leading to the house. As they labour through this insane flood and into the house, the staircase beckons with sanctuary until they eventually reach its first few steps and climb to the upper levels. What transpires in the upstairs rear chamber is inevitable.

Yvette's awakening by a remote and alien figure is, psychologically speaking, something which she herself caused to happen, for that raw impersonal force abides within her unconscious and signals the way towards a relationship with the world of masculinity. However, as is typical of the animus, when Yvette awakens later she finds that he has disappeared. Unfortunately we are not permitted to discover whether any relationship develops between Yvette and the gypsy, for at this point the story is left hanging in mid-air. One could conjecture that in the aftermath of this symbolic purifying of alien values and the resultant exposure to powerful masculine energies, she might begin to perceive some of the realities of her inner psyche. This could occur through relationship with her gypsy lover, or simply through the dawning realisation that she, the erstwhile virgin, is somehow no longer the same person.

A contemporary example of the unworldly fascination with the love object is seen in the 1950s film *Yield To The Night*, with Diana Dors' portrayal of a woman under the spell of the animus, condemned to death, for the murder of her rival in love. The protagonist, Mary Hilton, is drawn into an indecently obsessive relationship with a man who neither loves nor cares for her, yet nonetheless retains the key to her heart. However, the man in question is similarly attracted to another woman who has captured *his* anima, thus engendering an unconscious ménage à trois. It is Hilton's ardent infatuation with this man that forces her to cling to the daydream that life will one day be restored to its former glory. But has it been glorious?

In the early stages of their liaison she sets herself up as female worshipper of her handsome prince, allowing herself to fall in love with aplomb. She is consequently prey to the most tantalising and provocative illusions an individual is ever likely to experience. Her love object is unable to return to her the same affections that she showers upon him, since he has emotions invested elsewhere. She refuses to let go, her animus makes it temporarily impossible to do so.

The dramatic intensity of *Yield To The Night* captures the effects of negative animus projection most tellingly. It serves as a metaphor for what may happen when attachment to the ideal love object, and its attendant illusory effect, is swollen out of realistic proportion. In the film, Mary Hilton spends her last night awaiting the hangman's noose for her crime of passion, the murder of the 'other woman'. Those jilted in love are often keenly aware of another kind of condemned cell when no attempt is made to relax the possession by one's internal emotions. The four walls surrounding Mary as she waits to die symbolise the walls of depression which close in upon the person who has loved and lost. It is the realisation that one has erred in the choice of partner, that one must abandon the dream and begin anew, which proves so frustrating, intensely painful, and even humiliating. Perhaps a few retraced steps will show that one had, after all, placed the love object too high on the pedestal, or at least fashioned an all too unrealistic picture. An inner wounding of this kind seems to offer no hope, and one must relinquish the obsession and start all over again at some later date. The hardest lessons we have to learn are about ourselves. The trials in the school of life, if we are to be truly educated, depend upon our capacity for self-awareness. Sometimes, a painful relationship experience with another is the only way of arriving at such awareness.

CHAPTER 6

BE YOUR OWN PROPHET

'The central thesis of the Western Mysteries is that the primal spirit creates outer reality through imagination. In the individual this has the most dramatic expression in the prophetic insight which causes time and events to coalesce.'
R.J. Stewart (*The Mystic Life of Merlin*)

Thus spoke Mr Stewart in his account of the twelfth-century biography of Merlin by Geoffrey of Monmouth. In his interpretation of the *Vita Merlini* (Life of Merlin), he asserts that Merlin's predictions have little or nothing to do with causality. It is not *he* who has determined the events he has seen, for the individual is merely the recipient for the 'spiritual and imaginative matrix that transcends the serial perception of time; the matrix that creates both the "event" and the "seeing" of the event.' This description of inner space, I understand to be analogous to Rainer Maria Rilke's suggestion that the future enters into us (in order to transform itself) long before it happens. It must somehow move through a period of gestation, in a kind of timeless unconscious womb before birth is given to the actual, physical event. Yet these esoteric reflections are a far cry from the popular conceptions of prophecy and seership, and have much more in common with the art of visualisation I shall be coming to in the next chapter.

The Pygmalion myth we encountered in the previous chapter embodies also a profound esoteric technique that is (most likely) scarcely used: the magickal attraction of one's 'love object' via the use of the imagination. Pygmalion's inner creation (though embodied in an outer object) of his *own* ideal woman is a most poignant act, but what I will *not* be advocating is the use of unconscious powers in order to attract some actual person known to you. The 'love spells' cast in this work owe their power to a direct relationship with the inner archetypes, the anima and animus. They work to beckon an individual towards the visualiser, an individual who is an appropriate embodiment of the inner ideal. Hence, this method has nothing at all to do with 'contagious' magick (see Chapter Seven), an archaic technique employed on the basis of physical association (as a direct psychic link) with the person towards whom the spell is directed.

The mantic arts, from the Greek *manteira*, meaning divination, have not at all times been considered as a means of inner psychological inquiry. Magick itself, as history tells us, has often been employed for slightly less than noble intentions. It is perhaps lamentable that even in the enlightened twentieth century, the occult is so pathetically misrepresented and still carries with it the aura of malice and dark deeds which it bore in the Middle Ages, described as ' . . . some devilish or curious art, revealing things secret, or foretelling things to come, which the Devil hath devised to entangle and snare men's souls withal to damnation.' Then again, an Elizabethan church minister's attitudes towards such shadowy acts being what they were, I suppose one could not readily expect any other kind of pronouncement. Much of the West's resistance of the 'foretelling of things to come' is because it is unable to shake off Christian religious dogma. Its tenets are deeply ingrained into the collective unconscious of Occidental society. The individual from the West rarely fails to resonate deep within to the sacred images portrayed by Mother Church, which, as we already are well aware, has gone to great lengths to condemn anything suggestive of the occult world.

The religious or materialistic person's outrage aimed at the curious art is fashioned from an unconscious collective response. This was grown during the times when we tortured witches with sharp instruments, or indeed any hapless mortal accused of practising sorcery. There are those who continue to wave the flag for Jesus in the most moralistic and zealous manner. Their reactions to astrology and the like are laced with as much fear as the hardened materialist's response to the unknown. The irrational response is based (however unconsciously) on fear.

The search for inner truth will prevail despite Christianity's claim that its teachings always have and always shall be the one and only, ultimate doctrine. Ironically perhaps, the many 'false prophets' of which we are warned in the New Testament have been rearing their heads in the name of Jesus himself, a great majority of them appearing around the beginning of the century, and the most established of them probably doing great business. I refer to the numerous religious cults, all of which claim absolute truth for their teachings. These may range from the pseudo-orthodox and pious, to edicts displaying unconventionality. For instance, the founder of the holy sounding 'Children of God' is on record as having written, 'We have a sexy God and a sexy religion . . . with a sexy following' which is quite obviously a proper and fitting enough reason to exhort female disciples to roam the streets in search of more eager converts: 'There's no reason not to display the blessing of the Lord . . . don't be afraid to wear low-cut gowns . . . no bras, see-through blouses, show them what you've got – that's the bait.' Thus at one end of this religious spectrum we have cult leaders encouraging their female flock to disclose their breasts in public, and at the other, the fundamentalist Christians with not one but two enemies – the aforementioned sects encroaching upon the Bible and, presumably, adapting it to suit their own purposes, and the occult fraternity supposedly doing the Devil's work.

It is through religion that we bear witness to the age-old phenomenon of god-projection. This is the externalisation of an unseen and unknown force, which becomes an objective divine entity, often shouldered with the unenviable responsibility of governing the affairs of man. It is our sense of impotence in a hostile world which determines the need for faith in something outside of the individual. Yet, as I shall demonstrate later, the world, God, reality, life, exists only for us according to how we create it: a world wrought from a very subjective reality indeed. From this viewpoint, the type of prophet referred to in this chapter's title is the result of the individual's determining what will happen 'to him' or 'to her' through the silent, creative powers of the psyche. As a result, he or she may have little use for the dogma of religion as the individual is exposed to the realities of the soul. As Freud once perceptively remarked, 'A turning away from religion is bound to occur with the fatal inevitability of a process of growth.'

It is with the Aquarian Age that we are witnessing the slow reversal of the god-externalisation phenomenon. The 'growth movement', for example, is determined to claim back those energies hitherto projected upon a divine agency, and place the individual again at the centre of his universe. What this implies is not a rejection of God, but a re-focusing of the relationship between the individual and the energies of the cosmos. That which exists without, exists also within, that is the human psyche. However, the trail to the hidden psyche is a path well worn by various travellers from previous ages. We must tread carefully if we are to avoid the same pitfalls which awaited previous occult wayfarers (*Experimental Magic*, Aquarian Press, 1972):

> The magical edifice has a glitter which fascinates the mind and can quickly overcome it altogether. Any unprejudiced reading of the medieval grimoires for instance, will reveal a depth of pathology that is truly staggering. Yet even today those grimoires can still claim their lunatic adherents.

The chasm between the strict rationalist and the 'lunatic adherent' is in the process of being narrowed. The Aquarian

Age has produced works by a new breed of spokespeople, highly perceptive writers unencumbered by Victorian superstition and credulity, religious dogma, or the fixed 'world-as-it-is' attitude of classical physics – writers such as the late Paul Brunton, David Conway, Isaac Bonewits and J.H. Brennan. Yet, if a little knowledge is not intrinsically a dangerous thing, it is most certainly a misleading one, and on that well-travelled path – the preoccupation with things hidden – perhaps a little prudence, if not a little healthy scepticism, is in order. Such a preoccupation is reflected in the popular interest in matters psychic, the growing number of groups and societies founded upon esoteric studies, the appearance of the 'psychic fair', the resurgence of occult lore, and in particular, the ever expanding 'psychic consultancy' business. In the Age of Aquarius it even appears that we are making some progress in resolving life's mysteries, for Nature does not seem *quite* so jealous of her secrets as she used to be. If, as the Greek philosopher Heraclitus once told us, Nature loves to hide, then she apparently has less places in which to do it.

In the modern day occult market place, today's scryer goes under the more palatable epithet of 'Tarot Consultant', 'Psychic Reader', or 'Hand Analyst'. Unsurprisingly, there are those sincere in their attempts at consciousness raising and the divining of occult knowledge, and those with an obvious lack of regard for the essence of the mantic arts. All are compensated by its commercial benefits – 'fortune tellers', armchair magicians promising instant success with the least effort possible, even advertising in-depth character revelation through computerised palmistry. On the receiving end are those, for instance, who will enlist the aid of their local seer expecting to be told when their luck will change, as they enter the consulting room with the conditions, 'If there's anything bad, you know, I don't want to hear it.' This is symptomatic of an age that can produce instant coffee, pain killers, electric light and brain-wave reproductions. It similarly demands instant life forecasts in the same manner that the meteorological office issues its outlook on the weather.

The general lack of wisdom regarding the inner worlds is further evinced in the dabblers in so-called Black Magic, who continue to affirm the layman's impression of the occult as blasphemous Satan worship accompanied by revolting animal sacrifices. Consequently, the aims of modern Magick remain misconstrued, particularly when one considers such images projected by newspaper reports of yet another disaffected youth bearing the psychological scars of 'Black Magic', or the so-called 'High Priest of the Temple' who is exposed as a formerly convicted childsex offender.

Our Magickal Ancestor – The Figure of Merlin

The quest for secret, often forbidden knowledge, is an archetypal motif pervading human evolution, yet it is a unique minority who throughout history have dared tamper with the Fates and set themselves up as defiers of 'that which has been written'. Such are the historical figures from the occult hall-of-fame, and to which the New Age philosophies owe their debt. In beholding the figures in this eternal museum one discovers the great philosophers, sages, magicians, mathematicians, poets, artists and astrologers. All of them share one pertinent characteristic, that of daring to question the ultimate nature of the world in which we exist. These often starkly contrasting individuals – some with a sincere purpose towards goodwill and the betterment of mankind, some basking in the limelight of their own inflated vanity – also declared that the transformation of life stems from the powers inherent within the human mind. For instance, occultist Cornelius Agrippa (1486-1535) wrote: ' . . . with his intelligence, his imagination, and his soul, [man] can act upon and transform the whole world.'

The twentieth-century, American writer, Napoleon Hill, provides the modern equivalent: 'It is said that man can create anything he imagines. All the "breaks" you need in life wait within your imagination.'

On having made the journey across the span of time, from the pre-Christian era's apocryphal Hermes Trismegistus, patron of the magical arts (most likely a powerful mythic image of the Magician), through to Roger Bacon of the thirteenth century (a man of great erudition, though jailed on charges of heresy) and arriving at the similarly derided figure of Aleister Crowley, the notorious 'Great Beast', we find our common thread in seekers after the truth.

The Aquarian Age seeker gravitates towards those subjects which might be collectively entitled the New Age philosophies. These are old age philosophies given new breath in a new era. A brief perusal of your local bookstore will reveal the extent to which the explosion of popular interest on such subjects has occurred. One can now browse through material on the I Ching, astrology, numerology, graphology, tarot cards, rune stones, palmistry and cartomancy, among a proliferation of other related subjects that, if requested in popular bookstores perhaps forty years ago, may have caused a few raised eyebrows from the kindly shop assistant. These days, the expanse can be seen very clearly indeed; if one examined the retail outlets which deal specifically with occult works one would discover works ranging from reincarnation to medieval history; early Christianity to Black Magic; Druidic ritual to Mahayana Buddhism; Witchcraft to Egyptology, to name but a few.

The human longing for secret wisdom may be traced to the primitive shaman, the medicine man of ethnic tribes whose ascension into induced ecstacy produced a transforming effect upon his consciousness. Yet we need not look so far away from home for our magickal roots, not even to the mid-European figures such as Paracelsus and Ficino, for an ancestral symbol. The twentieth century's search for esoteric knowledge is rooted in British soil. In many ways the Father of the Western mystery tradition, Merlin is a figure who represents the psyche's underlying motivation towards growth and transformation. There are many cross references from early historical texts, and a multitude of logical connections available to be made with regard to the 'genuine' sixth-century seer.

We are advised in the *History of the British Kings* by Geoffrey of Monmouth, of the birth of a prophet in South Wales. The birth is the result of circumstances befitting all good myths, for Merlin was conceived from the union of a virgin and an other-worldly being. It is from this meeting of the earthly and the spiritual that he derives his multifaceted nature (something which we shall explore more fully later). Consequently, as a fully grown man he is both inspired wise prophet and wild man of the forest, the Lord of the Animals. Merlin embraces a whole host of mythic themes and, appropriate to his role as the 'shape shifter', cannot ultimately be reduced to one central identity. He comes to us in a variety of disguises: as Trickster, Shaman, Wise Prophet, Wild Man, Christ, Anti-Christ and revered Magus.

What is his significance for us as the prototype of the magician? Symbolically speaking, he represents the human power to create, though to embrace the meaning of this, one must first apprehend what is indicated by the word 'create'. By this I refer to the influence of willed thought upon its environment, appearing literally to bring forth certain desired phenomena. However, before we undertake to study the symbolism deeper, Merlin may be understood as the human power of self-awareness, creativity and wisdom.

From various historical sources – though it is from the mythical angle that I am approaching the figure of Merlin – we learn that the Prophet is involved with the setting up of the Table Round. This is either an epithet for an affiliation of knights, or an actual circular table which Merlin constructed for King Arthur's father, Uther Pendragon. One of the most prevailing opinions, although certain old texts provide variations, is that the table was attended by twelve knights. Here is where we dive into a pool of symbolic associations.

If we look at the symbolism of the circle (the Table Round) and the number twelve (the number of knights), we may see more clearly the threads of myth woven into the outer garment of an apocryphal historical event. The circular table at which the dozen knights sit is redolent of a complete and integrated system, the circle without beginning or end, signifying eternity and everlastingness. From the psychological standpoint it is the most adequate way of portraying the psyche in graphic form. Indeed, it is represented in precisely this way via mandala symbolism, of which the horoscope wheel is a prime example with its twelve zodiac signs, a complete cycle of human development. The zodiac is also intrinsic to the twelve solar months which, according to Tom Chetwynd's *Dictionary of Symbols* (Paladin, 1982), are 'symbolically related to life and the life's work'. It depicts a whole cycle of nature which must begin anew after the last stage is complete. When we internalise this 'table' we find a correspondence in the cyclical growth-decay patterns in human development. The key figure is Merlin, who fashioned the Table Round at the very beginning, and who points the noble chevaliers of Britain towards the quest for the Holy Grail. Through the wizard Merlin we have a connection between the Knights of the Round Table and the mythical Grail Quest, the search for one's true, inner Self.

Consequently, one must regard the Table Round and the Grail as components of the same mythic theme. The former, with its 'twelve' symbolism, represents the Wheel of Life, a cycle of the 'life's work', the ego's round journey within the circumference of all possible experience. The latter is an image of the Self, the inner jewel, the final spiritual core of one's being. It is no accident that the astrological glyph for the sun – depicting one's true essence – is a dot (the inner jewel?) enclosed within a circle. Hence, Merlin acts here, in his most universal capacity, as the psyche instinctively driven to seek out its inner origin and true nature, to arrive at its 'centre'. This feat cannot be achieved without the lengthy, round and often perilous journey through outer life. Though to 'find oneself' may be the ultimate goal in life, it cannot be done without taking the first step on the path, upon the Wheel of Fortune, the first tentative step to becoming aware of the world and oneself.

The wizard Merlin stands behind one of the greatest of archetypal mysteries, the cursed blessing of self-awareness. In the act of fashioning the Table Round and the institution of the Holy Quest, he not only has foreknowledge of man's far reaching journey through life and apparent knowledge of future events, but he intervenes to assist the mortal at various points on the road towards self-realisation. And awareness is the primary goal of the magician, for with that knowledge of the Self he may then continue along the occult path armed with working tools with which to transform both inner and outer worlds.

One may find a symbol of such use of the powers of mind in the Major Arcana of the tarot deck, in the card of the Magician. Here is depicted a youthful male standing before a table upon which are placed four magical implements symbolising the four elements, the prime archetypal forces of the universe. He has one arm raised above the head, pointing towards heaven, and the other pointing down towards the earth in an apparent act of drawing some spiritual force on to the physical plane. It is an image which suggests a confident understanding about life. It illustrates the individual at the stage of development where he or she has acquired a certain degree of mastery over the elemental forces within. The individual has at least affected a general 'rounding out' of character, as we witness the pictorial Magician presiding over and governing the elemental forces in and around him. There is also an allusion to the 'knowledge is power' axiom. With developing awareness of the rhythms of life – psychic and physical – and the relationship between them, one may take the reins of the will and employ that intuitive knowledge in a practical way.

The four 'tools' laid upon the table of the Magus (in some versions he is called the Juggler) are symbolic objects related to the four elements: the wand (Fire), pentacle (Earth), sword (Air), and chalice (Water), lie before him as key associations with the psychic forces, which he has learned successfully to integrate. Also, the Magus card denotes the arrival at a special point of knowledge in relation to the psyche and environment, as its divinatory meanings will duly indicate: skilfulness, power of the will in operation, ability to realise creative potential, cleverness, adeptness and sleight of hand. The latter characteristic, with its implications of guile, connects Merlin the Magician with the mythic figure of Hermes, the brilliant and ingenious communication god from the Greek pantheon on Mount Olympus, notorious for his trickery and cunning mental dexterity. However, there exists a more profound aspect to Hermes than mercurial cleverness. It is Hermes among the gods who bears the Caducaeus, a staff around which are entwined two serpents, one dark one light. These two symbolise the positive-negative polarity which pre-empts all manner of creation. Moreover, since the serpents are complementary to one another they together form a whole, an everlasting process, a motif also exemplified in the symbol for eternity (∞) suspended above the head of the Magician in certain versions of the tarot. The serpent is an ancient representation of inner wisdom, specifically related to the forces of the unconscious.

The Caducaeus, with its twin reptilian forces, refers to the knowledge of both outer and inner worlds, conscious and unconscious, material and psychic, mundane and magical. Hermes, as the bearer of this staff, is not only at large in the everyday affairs of the world (conscious mind), he is also to be found journeying to the Underworld (unconscious) as courier to the souls of the dead. Thus the Hermes-Merlin archetype represents one of the most sublime facets of the human psyche.

Further study of Merlin, will reveal that he portrays many different facets of the workings of the psyche. For our purposes in regard to creative transformation, he must become what Tom Chetwynd has termed a 'compressed symbol', by which is meant a symbol that is limited in meaning by the intellect so as not to merge with other similarly related material. For instance, as the prototype of the Magician he embodies the power of reason, the force of the intellect, and the cerebral skills that are necessary to gain control of the emotions (Water/Chalice), engage the will into action (Fire/Wand) and appreciate the passage of time on the physical plane (Earth/Pentacle), through which his spells must manifest and come to fruition.

The symbolic object representative of this force is the Sword, the power of intellect that cuts through the mass of undifferentiated thought in order to arrive at a clearly defined expression. It is the 'one-pointedness' of thought, bearing a finite meaning. It creates the world of opposites and polarities by dividing the 'object' into two halves. Black and white, evil and good, day and night become sharply contrasted. Such differentiation is for the purpose of cognition and apprehension since one thing is defined by virtue of its polar opposite, what it is 'not'. Presiding over this universal intention we can discover the figure of Merlin in a tale couched in the language of medieval myth.

I refer to the ennobling test of strength which Merlin arranges for the young Arthur in order that he shall prove his legitimacy as heir to the throne of England, the event of the Sword and the Stone. Arthur must withdraw a sword (in some versions of the legend identical to the magical Excalibur) which is firmly embedded in a large rock. Viewed symbolically, it depicts the will of Merlin (the self-motivating psyche) as requiring from the young king-to-be (developing ego), the separation from and eventual raising of mental power above the plane of earthly instincts and 'lowly' everyday matters. This must happen if the mind is ever to acquire the degree of strength necessary to the magical act. When the intellect has been sufficiently liberated from the habitual concerns of the 'lower' mind, from the bondage to negative subconscious patterns or the glorification of the senses, then, and only then, may it operate effectively. This is what the symbolic separation of the Sword from the Stone seems to imply.

Now we turn to another 'compressed symbol' which forms

the next stage in the use of magical powers, an object found in possession of the Magician of the Tarot trumps, the Wand. As a representative of the Fire element it denotes the power of the magical will in action, the expression of personal identity, one's essential 'beingness'. It personalises the objectivity and cold sharp reason of the Sword. If the Excalibur symbolises the power of rational thought over the environment then the magical wand sees that thought energy imbued with definite purpose, geared emotionally. Such emotions, necessarily under control, are directed towards the ritual act, and thus embody the concentrated will of the magician. Such 'magical will', the transformative power of thought, is allegorised in the popular image of the magician/wizard. One need look no further than the veteran of many children's stories, the wizard bearing a wand with which he is able to change one thing into another. Obscured by the almost comic persona of the white-bearded old wizard/magician/sorcerer complete with wand and book of spells, is the fact that thought energy under the control of the will, as symbolised in the wand, holds the power to perform a remarkable transformation of events and situations in one's life. Thus caricatured in the wand, it can produce certain results, magically and instantly.

Our purpose now is to use this knowledge in the field of human relationships in the preparation of a love spell worthy of Merlin himself!

LOVE SPELLS
PART TWO
PRACTICE MAKES PERFECT

CHAPTER 7

WHEN I DREAM –
VISUALISING A LOVER

Perhaps the use of love philtres and potions throughout the ages, and their association with profane, cackling old witches, has successfully reduced the perception of the magickal spell to that of nonsense. The wretched hag, as she presides over the cauldron dropping in the most unimaginable and potently inedible ingredients, is an image well entrenched within the collective psyche. Yet behind the seemingly crude masquerade lies the idea of correspondence, of symbolic alikeness, the axiom of like attracting like. 'Love spells' from certain branches of the magickal crafts would comprise of, amongst other items, say, a lock of hair or nail clippings of the person selected as the object of the ritual. By performing such an apparently trivial ceremony with the erstwhile physical extensions of the desired love object, the unsuspecting person might then be drawn to the one desirous of capturing the heart of the 'beloved'. What is at work here is a symbolic, though nonetheless real link with the object. In appropriating for use such a thing as a lock of hair or a piece of clothing, one makes contact with the 'energies' of that person, a psychic contact.

It might seem strange that I should commence a discussion on the art of visualising with reference to the paraphernalia of the sorcerer. Yet, as we have seen in the symbolism concerning Merlin, one must not confuse the outer apparel with the psychic forces they represent. In this context, the symbolic lock of hair is no less potent an object than the concentrated mental image in the mind of the visualiser. Both are representations of a particular kind of energy, the former as a physical symbol, the latter, a mental one. To work 'love magic', in this case to attract one's inner ideal love partner, consequently requires some definite kind of symbolic apparatus, a property that one already possesses in the 'form' of the imagination, the projected mental image. This particular technique may be employed to assist the individual in taking the first step forward towards the realisation of some cherished desire, towards something he or she has longed for or encountered frustration in achieving, the experience of love. But first things first, what is 'visualisation', and moreover, why should one want to perform such a practice in the first place?

To begin with, a definition: creative visualisation is the art of creating mental images in order to transform the inner or outer world of the individual. Such images are put to use in what might loosely be described as a ritual, whereby the individual powerfully imagines him or herself actually in possession of the thing so desired, participating in the inner mental drama where he or she already 'has' that longed for object. By invoking feelings to such a pitch whereby the inner images assume an almost objective reality (they appear to exist independently of the visualiser), one is somehow held captive by the 'reality' of them. This marks the emergence of a subtle and mysterious unconscious process, the transmutation of mental energy into its physical equivalent. Indeed, as one writer has succinctly pointed out, 'when you have it, it has you'. When one reads somewhere that the world of images tends to reproduce itself in material form, or that the environment is a looking glass, one is bearing witness to the echoes of a profound, age-old reality, that the world is ultimately a manifestation of Mind.

Whether or not Joe Layman knows it, he is unconsciously planting the seeds of future events with every moment of every thought since experiences at external levels are a reflection of his inner self. Moreover, there is no fundamental distinction between physical reality (outer world), and psychic reality (inner world), both being different manifestations of the same energy. The implication is perhaps disturbing here to some people. It hangs responsibility for what happens to them mostly upon *their* shoulders. Perhaps the injunction at Delphi to 'Know Thyself' ought to be lengthened to include ' . . . for thou createth thine own universe.' This axiom is mirrored in events usually held to be insignificant, from the manner in which the pompous shop assistant treats you, to exasperation at being unable to find a clean shirt, to experiencing blind rage at the 'engaged' tone for the fourth time, attempting to get through to the local taxi rank.

Such events experienced as coming from without are themselves reflections of unconscious tensions (i.e. the withholding of energy) appearing as a physical event. We are creating what happens to us in quite a real sense indeed. The psychic atmosphere that one carries almost guarantees its recreation in the external world. As Prentice Mulford indicates (*Thought Forces*, Bell and Hyman, 1979): 'It is the mood of mind that you are most in, whether that be grovelling or aspiring, that is actually making physical conditions of life in advance for you.' All that is required of the non-initiate of visualisation is an apprehension of this self-same thing. Imagine then, what would happen were one to revolutionise one's whole manner of thinking, and to concentrate upon, intensely and repeatedly, that ideal future in one's imagination – a tomorrow spent with one's potential love partner?

At this stage it is worth emphasising once more that the impulses of thought-energy are continually manifesting themselves and seeking expression in the life of an individual. A concentrated visualisation ritual is a potent embodiment of such energy. By imbuing one's hopes, dreams and longings with this force we actually avail ourselves of a channel through which they may eventually emerge. Such aspirations, through the technique of mental imagery, become a highly concentrated and magnetic 'form' of energy.

Provided that our faith in the powers of mind is strong enough, the forces peculiar to the imagination are guarantee enough that one's 'love magic' shall work. But why the use of such forces in order to attract a partner?

The first answer I would call to mind is that, for the layman, the technique sounds like an attractive 'get something for nothing with the aid of mind-power'. Such an attitude may apply equally to the person merely toying with the idea of 'having' a relationship, or the individual who profoundly recognises that, emotionally, something is missing from his or her life. However, one is labouring under a mental blind spot in entertaining the idea that visualisation equals something to be had for nothing. The ritual invocation and projection of mental energies encompasses the necessary preparation, effort, and not just a little discipline. This standard framework notwithstanding, we must now question the motives of the individual who sincerely *does* wish to meet a partner, and who realises that a certain amount of psychological work is required. Here we are not questioning the use of visualisation as a potent and convenient method, but the end to which it is directed.

Perhaps our hypothetical subject simply believes that as soon as the mystery person appears in their life, unending bliss will prevail and both can live happily ever after, in short, that the arrival of the partner automatically spells happiness. Indeed, for the first few weeks, months, even years, this may prove to be the case. Yet somewhere along the line some effort will be required to acknowledge the inner foundation upon which such a relationship is built, especially with regard to the disturbances created by the anima and animus. This does not imply a pessimistic view. It means that a successful 'love spell' is not to be treated as an end in itself, for a relationship – as a union and continuous interplay of male and female energies – is hardly a static thing and requires time and effort for it to 'work'. One's love relationship is not a trophy to be hung over the fireplace and admired from afar, much less an everlasting magical dream. It is a fact of life, an entity through which each partner can come to terms with each other's and their own individuality, a learning experience.

Buried beneath the reasons given for wanting to attract someone into one's life lies the human need to love and be loved, an urge deeply rooted within the sphere of the emotions. The tendency to pursue relationships as a means of 'security' is the need to stabilise oneself on a feeling level. It is most often the individual's emotional security that is at stake. For example, observe the individual, who behaves in an apparently insensitive and nonchalant way towards their partner, transform into a disoriented case of tears and grief if ever that partner should abandon them.

Both sexes are often convinced, with an obstinacy that a nuclear missile could not disturb, that the 'ideal lover' is to be found somewhere out there among the grey ambience of ordinary life. Yet our technique need not prove disillusioning. On the contrary, it is one of the begetters of the individual's emergence into the world of conscious awareness, if only it was realised that the dreamy apparition of the true lover is a picture of one's own unconscious, or more appropriately, of the anima or animus. One hears or reads, time and time again, of those destroyed souls who, in search of love and romance, have had their hearts split in two by the prince or princess that turned out to be less than regal, or of those who have given up the struggle entirely, disclosing that they are always unlucky in love. Such disappointments are a consequence of being quite unaware of the nature and origin of the projected archetype, the projection of the anima or animus into the external world. As a preliminary to visualisation, we must now turn our gaze inwards to discover that our magical prince or princess is a product of the invisible, unconscious psyche.

For those with an already fertile imagination this ought to prove relatively easy, and for those without, some work will be necessary in encouraging the image-making faculty. One rather obvious preparation is in order, namely that of finding an undisturbed place in which to work. At the outset of your exploration of inner space, you will soon realise that the formation of arbitrary images is occurring all the time. We must take up Merlin's Wand and employ it to focus the mind upon a particular image. To do this will require some practice.

Working with one's ideal love-image encompasses the need to 'see' them as convincingly as one might study one's reflection in a mirror or a pool of water; observe the shape of the head, colour of hair and eyes, facial expressions and the like, an ideal being created with the inner eye. With sufficient effort you will eventually discover that an unconscious mechanism comes into play to assist in strengthening and clarifying the image. No matter how difficult this exercise may at first seem, you must persist up to the level whereby the visualisation acquires a life all of its own, as one's hitherto practised images become a natural habit. When the picture of the anima/animus has developed into a reality, you may then stage the mental scenes that you wish to realise in the outer world.

A second component of this mental theatre is the realm of the emotions, which in the ritual proper are the required accompaniments to 'getting through' to the unconscious mind. As Al Koran firmly states in *Bring Out The Magic In Your Mind*, 'Seeing and feeling are necessities.' One may expand on the analogy of theatre productions quite effectively. That is how the visualised scenes may appear to the individual, although in this production one is simultaneously producer, director, scriptwriter, actor and audience. Let us suppose that you imagine yourself and your lover walking home on a rainy day. As you approach the front door reaching for your key, a blazing log fire is awaiting your presence in the cosy ambience of the living room. As 'director' and 'producer' you will be manipulating the scene with as much realism as your imagination can muster, bringing your idealised romance to life on the film set in your mind's eye. With enough persuasion your unconscious will start to react as if it were actually taking place. You will respond with the appropriate emotions. It is mostly in the role of actor/audience that the transformative power emerges. As you intently observe the action occurring in your inner theatre you will, by necessity, invoke strong and dramatic emotions in acknowledgement of the visualised scenes, as you witness yourself participating in the inner drama. It is perhaps difficult to discern in this context whether you are truly actor or audience. In such a ritual there is a convergence of subject and object since in those emotionalised moments of imagery, the actor upon the 'stage' is no less real than the audience observing the action. This experience is poetically described in Indian mythology, at the pinnacle of emotional intensity, as the dancer becoming the dance.

In opening the door to one's spontaneous emotional reactions, inviting this mentally-crafted attractive phantom into the imagination as a permanent guest, one may be forgiven for thinking that this is an escapist, self-indulgent fantasy. This is the point at which the ego must give up its habit of attempting to control and make objective sense of the world 'out there'. It is asked to acknowledge a greater power, though unfortunately one which cannot be experienced directly. When the visualisations are developed with the requisite effort and enthusiasm, and above all one puts *faith* into those images, then certain universal laws regarding the nature of attraction come into play. Visualisation, to be successful, rests as much upon beliefs of the individual as it does on practising imagery and the evoking of emotions. In reference to this I quote the wonderfully direct maxim of Al Koran: 'The stronger you feel about something, the sooner it is going to happen.' This indicates that some abstract entity (faith, conviction) colludes with the world to bring about results.

It has been my experience that the true power or governing force that is behind visualisation is the faith that it will work. To paraphrase J.H. Brennan, any magical ritual works in the direction of one's belief, and not necessarily one's intention.

Hence, one may be desirous of achieving certain results or of effecting a positive transformation of one's life, but the unconscious seems to have deaf ears to what the ego 'wants' unless the conscious mind actually believes, firmly and convincingly, that the desire will be realised. Any faith in the power of such rituals, and in the powers of Mind, must come directly from the heart of the individual.

An apparently retrogressive step is now required as a necessary constituent to effective visualisation. This somehow determines the measure of faith or belief one has in the powers of the unconscious mind. Paradoxically, it consists in forgetting all about the visualisation, that is, during usual everyday pursuits, during the times when one is not actually engaged in the ritual. The notion that one might in fact increase the powers of attraction (and thus bring the object nearer) by concentrating more and more upon the image during normal routines turns out to be false. The mind, bombarded with impressions from the environment, fleeting memories, and a host of other effects, cannot effectively make any further impression by simply recalling the memorised images. As we have seen, visualisation is more than simply the production of mental pictures. Thus the advice of the occultist is to 'let go' of the thought and to trust the unconscious successfully to operate its manifold and mysterious processes. The matter of belief enters into the situation here. One relinquishes control by the ego, and its questions of whether or not the visualisation will work, in good *faith* that the silent forces will bring about desirable results. Genuine acknowledgement is made that an unseen power is in the process of effecting the desired transformation. The unconscious is perpetually at work receiving the impressions and 'commands' of the ego, whether or not the ego apprehends this. Hence, to 'let go' is not to let go at all, but to allow one's request, the visualised image, to reach the ears of the unconscious, and to entrust 'it' with your desires. It will continue with the work you have hitherto carried out.

There are two common pitfalls at the onset of the magickal

journey. Visualisation almost always fails the person with an over-apprehensive attitude, whereby he or she will expect results delivered within a certain time-scale. It will also fail if there is a demand for mechanistic explanations as to the 'how' of mental imagery, an attitude not too distinct from doubt or scepticism. However, I believe there to be nothing fundamentally mysterious about the 'mechanics' of visualisation. If it can be truly appreciated that mind equals energy equals matter, and that one's psyche is a self-asserting dynamism, then it may dawn that the energies associated with the visualised images are at work somewhere, transforming themselves into the most appropriate channel of expression. The visualisation will manifest in its own good time, and though this may provoke anxiety on the part of the visualiser, this need not, and indeed should not, be so. When the imaged partner *does* eventually appear, the manifestation process will have come to its true conclusion, and there will be something altogether 'right' about the person you have attracted. Moreover, the apparent coincidences leading up to this coming together will be exposed as necessary links in the overall pattern. If one can turn a blind eye to the encroachment of scepticism and anxiety, one's visualisation will be allowed to flow freely, to find its replica at the material level. The ego has little authority in the matter at this stage. It ought not contort itself by worrying about the how and when of the 'mechanics' of the unconscious.

A True 'Love Spell'

For this section I will relate the experiences of a young man of my acquaintance (whom I shall call Carl). They illustrate the effects of mental imagery, and the way in which the unconscious appears magically to bring about appropriate results in the concrete world. It concerns an individual not unlike many other hopeful and aspiring souls in search of love, romance, and togetherness.

Two factors contributed to Carl's decision to employ

'mind-power' in order to attract a love partner with whom he could share his life: firstly there was his introduction to the 'occult fraternity', people with a passionate interest in New Age subjects; secondly, his erstwhile failed relationship from several months before. It had been approximately ten weeks since this break up, and Carl was only just beginning to get over the fact that a certain lady was no longer now in his life. Like so many other young men and women, he had experienced this loss as a bitter personal tragedy enveloped in the darkened hallways of despair. His pain served to firm up his resolve to find the 'right' one. Moreover, he had discovered the magical technique of visualisation.

Carl dedicated himself to furthering his knowledge of mental imagery and quizzed anyone versed in the subject in order to discover more about the wisdom of thought influence. It was during this period that he met up with a trusted and older astrologer friend of his, who, by the grace of Meaningful Coincidence, happened to impart the kind of reassuring advice that he sought. The astrologer friend, whom Carl respected as an individual with a profound knowledge of occult teachings, told him 'whatever you think, you will create', which is of course, precisely what Carl wanted to hear. When the pupil is ready, the teacher will appear. And thus did Carl engage himself in intense periods of ritual imagery.

However, five long months passed and his conscious mind seemed to serve only to remind him that the girl of his dreams, whom he had seen in scores of romantic scenarios, existed only in his head. What was occurring in his outer life at this time was not only incidental to his inner dreams but crucial to them. Shortly after the separation from his girlfriend, Carl had gone in search of employment, ostensibly to provide a diversion from the pull of the past and its attendant memories. With the commencement of a new job, having been previously unemployed, it was hoped that the change of environment and overall routine would occupy his thoughts and assist in the 'forgetting process' – as well as improve his finances. About two months later, he managed to secure a part-time position in an office answering telephone calls for an establishment that operated a transport service for the disabled. Yet, as the passage of time appeared to extend mercilessly into an unknown future, the thought occurred to him that he had still not yet encountered the enchanting female who appeared only to remain a creation of his mind. It did not matter that he could see and feel her when he closed his eyes, that she was *real*, nor that by now he was a visualiser *par excellence*. She had not yet been found 'out there'. Yet he knew without doubt that she must exist.

A little later, quite suddenly and without warning, with no intuitions or hunches as to when his dream was going to manifest, events in the material world began to take shape and Carl experienced what he calls his 'two near misses'. These were the natural consequence of mental forces projected into the environment, a much needed release of sorts. On two separate occasions he attracted the attentions of a female whom he at first believed was *the* one he had been waiting for. But as events later showed, neither female was much interested in him.

When one has willed something to happen so intensely over a long period of time, a series of 'near misses' in the material world indicates the working out of an inner process, as if the energies are at last transforming themselves into the appropriate end result. Or as Cicero succinctly put it: 'Certain signs precede certain events.' The unconscious had not yet discovered a suitable channel, the person and circumstances pertaining to the envisioned relationship. In the light of what had just transpired, it was understandably difficult for Carl to believe that his lasting relationship would ever materialise. As befits the limitations of conscious orientation, he could not discern an invisible pattern working itself out, a process that would eventually culminate in what he was looking for. Mind – as an intelligent principle lying behind the world of form – belongs to an invisible universe not detectable by the normal senses. It is a force whose results one only encounters second-hand in that we perceive only its *effects* in the phenomenal world of body and environment.

While we cannot directly observe the processes of the unconscious as they unfold, and thus have no direct knowledge of *any* process occurring, the occultist is at least assured that by taking certain preparatory steps in the psychic world, i.e., the enactment of ritual, a certain kind of result will occur in time, in the physical world. When those results do occur, they do so in an apparently random and arbitrary fashion, which is precisely how Carl felt about what happened next. A vacancy had recently arisen within the department for someone to assist the vehicle driver on his trips to various locations. Carl had long since grown tired of being confined to a desk for most of the day. The move was made possible because of an expansion programme within the company (and we shall discover the relevance of this later). This necessitated the opening of another premises, and extra staff were needed to maintain it. Carl soon found what he had been looking for when an almost instantaneous attraction (to him) was expressed by a woman who had been employed to run the small office rented by the company in their expansion programme. It is perhaps doubtful whether he would have discovered her at all had he not acted upon the impulse to take advantage of the new vacancy. This was a key factor. His new situation brought him into frequent contact with the new office, which is where he consequently met Sarah. What transpired within the space of two weeks is scarcely believable, and it convinced Carl that the mental universe holds the key to the future. He says that his relationship is too perfect a resemblance to that which he originally imagined, to ever doubt the powers of visualisation. 'The only thing wrong,' he reflects, 'is that she doesn't look anything like how I pictured her.'

What actually did happen in that subsequent short period may be likened to the sudden unravelling of an elastic band after having been wound many times over, or the faulty mechanism of a clock forcing the hands to accelerate as the inner spiral rapidly unwinds itself. The normal speed of events became increased. Within that short space of time, after their first date, the relationship had developed rapidly. Carl had moved out of his parents' house, secured the tenancy to a flat, and the two of them were living together as if they had known each other for years. It was not on a few occasions that Carl was heard to mutter: 'It's all happening so suddenly.' There was no 'getting to know each other', no gradual development of future plans; here was the relationship he had visualised 'happening to him' instantly.

This phenomenon occurs when the manifestation process has come to its true end, and has become, to borrow a metaphor, 'overripe'. At this point the visualisation is ready to yield fruit. When it does so on the material plane, it does so suddenly. These events came about quickly and within such a short space of time, because when the appropriate physical outlet, the meeting with Sarah, was 'found', phenomena on the material plane had rapidly to contain the previously stored energies and 'catch up' with the mental world, where this relationship already existed.

With hindsight, one can see that even apparently arbitrary events played their part in the successful conclusion of Carl's visualisation: the search for fresh employment, the consequent disillusionment with a boring office job, the 'chance' occurrence of an alternative position within the company, and the willingness to make that move. All of these were threads in the overall pattern leading to his eventual 'luck' in discovering the appropriate person. The terms 'chance' and 'luck' allude to a deeper, underlying reality than the one we are usually accustomed to. Considering the appropriateness of the manifested visualisation, there was some apparent intelligent force that 'knew' of the most available and apposite channel through which it could manifest. This intelligent 'something' placed Carl in the correct place at the correct time in order to see to it that his visualisation was successful. Such a collusion between the world of imagination and the world of matter is far from arbitrary. It indicates that the forces of will, emotion and conviction, when invested in visualisation, are sufficient to engage this apparent intelligence in the unconscious. They will reach out and arrange physical events in an orderly, sequential fashion. However one interprets this process, whether one postulates cause and effect, the natural immanence of mind and matter, or the answer to one's prayers, the invisible world of the psyche cannot refrain from discovering itself in the visible world of the material.

CHAPTER 8

A TEMPLE TO HEKATE

'Then to Phoebus and Trivia I will set up a temple of solid marble. Thee also a stately shrine awaits in our realm; For here I will place thy oracles and utterances.'
Virgil, The Aeneid

As Trivia, She of Three Ways, Hekate was venerated as the 'most holy prophetess who foreknowest the future' in ancient Rome as late as 19 BC. Earlier in Greece, she was afforded a much higher rank as a powerful underworld goddess who delivered up the wealth of the earth to those who worshipped her. In Euripedes' *Medea* in the fifth-century BC, the title character, a sorceress from Colchis, pays homage to her magickal patroness Queen Hekate, the goddess who is her 'chosen accomplice' and to 'whose presence [her] central hearth is dedicated.' For a deity of such immense power her mythology is sketchy, and Hekate rarely receives mention from the early Greek writers. However, this is in itself befitting of the nature of the Night Goddess. Like Hades, the Lord of the Underworld, she personifies a largely unknowable, enigmatic and hidden force in the universe. The goddess of Magick, divination, sorcery (and later witchcraft), was not to be seen in the pantheon upon Mount Olympus. She symbolises that unconscious power that brings about the desired physical conditions required by the one who has petitioned her. Appropriately, in acknowledgement of the archetypal feminine force, she is credited with power over the earth and

133

sea, granting riches and victory to mortals, be they farmers, soldiers, fishermen, sailors, athletes or bakers. She is also identified with the moon goddess Artemis/Diana, presiding over the female 'powers of night'. In this guise she would roam the countryside in her tricephalic form with her demonic accomplices, the hounds of hell. Darkness; Mystery; The Creative Process; Invisibility; Hidden Powers; all of these are universal *yin* forces. Thus it is a feminine deity I have chosen to represent the unconscious 'mechanics' of visualisation, as a complement to the conscious Magical Will of Merlin.

The denial of the gods is an important issue, since we have observed forces in the unconscious which behave in the same way. The appellation one gives to them is irrelevant, for it is a matter of human *experience*. Consequently, the Temple to Hekate you will erect is an acknowledgement of your own magickal 'goddess', or that archetypal feminine power which calls upon the forces of the universe. Such a temple is symbolic, though one should at all times treat seriously this workplace in the mind as She becomes your 'chosen accomplice'. The 'love spells' you will be performing are unique and individual efforts at attracting your own pre-existent *ideal* lover, the outlines of which have been discussed earlier. It is in this chapter that I wish to draw you closer, by presenting detailed techniques, which you can employ to set into motion the creative processes of the unconscious mind. Let us first look at some of the original contributors to the legacy of the magickal love spell.

From the pagan practices of the early centuries AD comes a particular rite designed to capture the heart of the Beloved. By today's standards this seems at best crude and unethical. It was the witchcraft of the early Saxons that introduced the 'love poppet', a kind of Western voodoo doll made from two identically (human) shaped pieces of fabric, sewn together and then stuffed with herbs. Naturally, this monstrous little device was intended to resemble the beloved one, whereupon the desirer would petition the help of one of the gods on his or her behalf. Also coming into usage around this period (fifth century AD) was the Mandrake, supposedly the oldest known narcotic plant in the history of botany, but also a prominent feature of the witch's paraphernalia. Its root is unique in that it resembles a human shape, hence its suitability in casting love spells. Much that is dark has been uttered about this (one time) insidious spume of the earth, indeed, the credulous minds of the Middle Ages seemed to be much in awe of its alleged diabolical power. According to one belief, anyone who dared pull up the Mandrake from the earth would die an instant death. In order to ward off such a drastic fate, anyone thus uprooting a Mandrake must, according to the tradition, 'tie a dog thereunto to pull it up, which will give a great shreeke at the digging up, otherwise if a man should do it he should surely die.'

In Germany it goes under the name of the Galgenmannchen (little gallowsman). This presumably accords with the legend that Mandrake are only to be found growing beneath a gallows where 'the matter that hath fallen from the dead body hath given it the shape of a man, the matter of a woman.' Thus relieved from the earth by said (now deceased) canine, it could be used as an ingredient in love philtres, perhaps measured with a carved wooden Love Spoon, or implemented in a magical rite dedicated to none other than Hekate.

Such were the beliefs prevalent among the occult-inspired populace of the Middle Ages. History has bequeathed us remnants of other pagan ceremonies even more base, and in many cases more unsavoury than those employing the Mandrake root. La Bibliothèque de l'Arsenal in Paris houses a considerable collection of occult treatises and magickal documents belonging to this period. Here can be discovered a work entitled the *Zekerboni*, which states that:

> To make oneself beloved there shall be taken, to wit, the heart of a dove, the liver of a sparrow, the womb of a swallow, the kidney of a hare, and they shall be reduced to impalpable powder. Then the person who shall com-

> pound the philtre shall add an equal part of his own
> blood; dried and in the same way powdered. If the
> person whom it is desired to draw into love is caused to
> swallow this powder . . . marvellous success will follow.

Another facet of this expansive diabolical legacy, in this case
an eighteenth-century French manuscript containing the
account *Segrets de magie pour se faire aimer* (Magic secrets for
making oneself beloved), boldly declares that:

> To gain the love of a person, rub your hands with the
> juice of vervain and touch the man or woman you wish
> to inspire with love.

In good Olde Englande, not too dissimilar practices were
undertaken by witches in accordance with the blithe folk-
belief that Mother Nature would yield her blessed secrets to
any old hag or crone. However, apart from those rites carried
out by the professional witch for the benefit of an ailing love-
sick 'client', the individual might perform certain ceremonies, with not one crushed animal innard in sight.

Such spells are to be found in a body of literature that was
discovered in the library of Samuel Pepys upon his death.
This was a collection of tiny chapbooks he had christened his
'Penny Merriments'. They were small, cheaply produced
pamphlets sold on street corners of the seventeenth-century,
reflecting the lives of commonfolk. Amongst the contents of
these chapbooks one might find ballards, broadsides, hu-
mour items, propaganda articles, and magickal spells. Thus
it is that we find an account, written in 1685, on the 'Rare
Secrets of Art and Nature; Tryed and Experienced by
Learned Phylosophers and recommended to all ingenious
Young Men and Maids'. The title of this mini-grimoire is
'Mother Bunch's Closet', the aforementioned good lady
being a well-known alewife in Elizabethan London. It is
supposedly in this closet that such infernal mysteries were
contained and then later discovered. Here we discover several ritual methods for attracting one's true lover. The first of
these is 'The Washing of the Smock on Midsummer's Eve',
which reads as follows:

> You that desire to know it this way must wait till Mid-
> summer Eve . . . must take your Smocks and dip them in
> fair water, then turn the wrong side outward and hang
> them on chairs before the fire, and have a vessel with
> drink in it . . . and in a little time the likeness of those
> persons you shall marry will come and turn your smocks
> and drink to you.

And another spell from 'Mother Bunch's Closet', entitled 'The sowing of Hempseed', instructs the performer of the ritual to enter into a place where there is grass growing, and with the right hand throwing said seed over the left shoulder, to pronounce: 'Hempseed I sow; Hempseed I sow; He that must be my true love come after me and mow.' On having repeated this eight times, the corresponding figure of the true love is then supposed to appear.

Many of the old love spells would have proven effective, simply because the lack of scientific regard for objective facts among such commonfolk permitted them to invest an extraordinary amount of faith into their rituals. The abstraction we have termed 'faith' is an extremely creative and powerful entity. Across the panorama of an individual's experience of life, it is the things one takes 'on faith', without recourse to reason or confining oneself to objective facts, which ultimately manifest in a positive end result. This is because the notion of failure never occurs. And whether or not this is seen as blind credulity or superstition, personal belief and the investment of 'reality' into an object or situation provides the object with an animating power not hitherto possessed by it.

What is real for me, need not necessarily be real for you. Consequently, the invocation of any archetype or god-force – provided that it is 'real' enough to the individual – is apt to assume a kind of quasi-personality infused with the inner energies of that individual. It is much the same with visualisation, except that no belief in an independent outside agent is necessary. The male employing mental imagery in order to attract his ideal woman merely calls upon and acquaints himself with the feminine forces of his psyche, his own anima. Getting to know it in this intimate way through successful visualisations not only puts him in touch with his 'female' side on the interior, but also on the exterior, as it were, for he will draw to him a woman exuding those qualities. Similarly, the female practitioner of visualisation encounters the imagined form of her ideal male, which is her animus.

Having plotted the general outlines of mental imaging in the previous chapter, I will now introduce the specific means for experiencing this process, for you may well be asking, 'What do I have to do in order to realise my dream?'

Firstly, one may have to surmount the mental barrier that mental imaging seems, on the surface, to be *doing* little at all. When such is the case it pays to remind oneself of the power of mental influence, and that willed thought is just as much an action as is something carried out physically, and no less practical or effective for that. To exert that influence we must allow the forces of mind to emerge from their half-slumber, and this necessitates an environment which permits solitude and tranquillity. It is then you will observe the need to calm the meandering train of thoughts, what Zen calls the 'monkey mind', in order to allow the unconscious to be heard. Thus rule one requires an undisturbed place where your ritual will suffer no distractions. (As a helpful note, one may find that if the place of ritual is in darkness, then the atmosphere is more conducive to visualising.) One may then proceed to visualise the temple, a temple which exists in nothing more strange or mysterious, than one's own consciousness.

Let us now take a look through the portals of the mind's eye, and attempt some basic techniques. Not everyone is blessed with the ability to capture immediately a clear, detailed mental image, and in this respect the following exercise will prove most helpful. Commence by making mental pictures of simple geometric designs such as a circle, square or triangle and practice 'holding on' to them in your mind's eye. When you are satisfied that these images are clear and substantial, expand upon this technique by affording these shapes three dimensions: create the images of spheres, cylinders, cubes or pyramids, and move them around in your imagination to reveal curvatures, opposite sides and perspective. Retaining these mental pictures may prove a little troublesome at first, for it is the tendency of the mind to lack a focus and by the retention of these images (something which one *must* master) you put your conscious will in charge.

However, the projected forms of your visualisation are as yet incomplete; they now require the added dimension of living colour. The importance of colour certainly ought to be borne in mind here, for, as far as the unconscious mind is concerned, it serves as a meaningful, symbolic gesture. Practise visualising (with closed eyes) an everyday object associated with a particular colour – an egg for instance – and change its colour to a less familiar one. A brown or white egg will be quite simple to imagine; transform it into a black one and capture that image for as long as it remains clear. Afterwards, visualise a different colour and retain that image also until you have a succession of different coloured eggs, blue, red, green, orange, purple, and so on.

The foregoing exercise is only one technique among many designed to stimulate contact with the world of images, and exercise one must, for the idea that practice makes perfect applies in this sphere no less than it does in any other. It is from this springboard that we may develop the techniques for modern love spells, since the visualisation of a love partner necessitates the experiencing of powerful animated images in the mind's eye. Let us first begin our love spell by visualising the facial features one finds most appealing, the characteristics that you respond to most readily in another. If you will persist in this practice, building up your thought form of desired hair colour, facial features, physical expressions (an attractive smile, for instance), you will have before you a mental image of a mysterious but appealing male or female, who is a pictorial representation of your unconscious. As your imaging ability gradually develops, the creative faculty of the inner mind will assist in fashioning the image spontaneously, bringing into play qualities in your imaginary partner that appear natural and 'right' to you. Eventually you will require less and less effort to construct the image, for then it will have become fixed in your memory and need only be recalled for subsequent rituals.

Crystal And Candle Visions

The following ritual may be performed with or without the aid of a crystal, but for those of you who already possess any of the varied forms of 'frozen light', such crystals will greatly enhance the performance of your ritual visualisation. One need only place a small piece of crystal in a closed palm of the hand to detect some physical sensation occurring that is unmistakably a result of the interaction between yourself and this apparently inert and lifeless form of matter. The intrinsic nature of matter is an *energy* field consisting of insubstantial sub-atomic particles whirling around in incessant frenzied motion. According to Ra Bonewitz, in his work *Cosmic Crystals*, the inner dynamics of these minerals remain in a perfect state of equilibrium, since the crystal both radiates and absorbs equal proportions of energy, and its basic atomic structure remains undisturbed. It is because of this harmonious state of affairs within the crystal, and its transformative properties (heat may be converted into electricity via the crystal, for instance) that the suitability arises for its use in mental imagery.

This leaves us with the matter of obtaining a particular crystal for use in ritual. You may like to check out those suppliers advertising in the New Age press who function as either mail-order outlets or retailers dealing directly with the public, and who provide a generous selection of stones, either set in jewellery or cut and ground, and sold as small pieces. Varieties such as Jasper, Venus Hairstone, Sodalite, Rose Quartz, Malachite, Tiger's Eye, Carnelian or Blue Lace Agate (to name but a few) are all stones which you may like to discover. *Any* crystal will assist in ritual work and possesses no unique occult powers of its own, independent of the user. If your magazine says that one particular crystal will bring you good fortune, prosperity and material wealth, and a different variety pertains to love, romance and family affairs, then one must first consider from where such information has been derived. Such objectification of the supposed individual properties of say, Rose Quartz compared to Black Onyx (or the association with a particular sign of the Zodiac), can be misleading since the efficacy of any particular crystal depends upon the personal energies of the individual, and the use of them thereof. Consequently, the crystal you select may be, as Ra Bonewitz puts it, 'programmed' and put to use in occult work tailored to a specific end. Moreover, it can be 'reprogrammed' when one is satisfied that it has served its purpose. For our purposes it is necessary only to employ the crystal as a focusing point for the release of mental energies during the actual ritual.

Take your crystal in either hand, and allow yourself to experience the sensation that arises. Accept this as a signal that your energy system is being activated and is passing through the crystal and around your entire body. You may like to visualise a circuit of energy travelling through your body, with a resultant aura of light emanating from it. The following visualisation may be carried out with, or without, a crystal, but such a talisman will almost certainly act as an energiser. With your eyes gently closed, having prepared for your ritual with a silent (preferably dark) room and a quiescent mind, you may thus begin to fill effectively your consciousness with the images you desire to see realised in the flesh.

Such projections may involve visualising yourself and your partner in an attractive environment, either totally imaginary or one actually known to you, enjoying each other's presence. Whatever pictures you choose to create, let them stimulate a feeling of positive, dramatic emotion. Simply feel good about the images before you. The choice of imaginary settings and activities is entirely up to you. Simply visualise yourself doing the things you would most love to do!

There is no time limit set to such a ritual, and with acquired experience you will probably continue until your inner energies appear to be exhausted. If you repeat the visualisation each day, not only will you bring the ultimate object of the exercise closer, but you will also be acquiring a skill. You will recognise this for yourself, for there is something graceful about a well-practised visualisation. The figures and situations perform most of the acting themselves in your mental theatre, creating the sensation that it is you who are the audience, feeling and responding to the action as it takes place. When you have reached such a level of ability, you may consider yourself a seasoned visualiser. The images now evoke a sublime feeling of intensity, rich meaningful depth, and above all, a reality.

Another useful and compelling focus is brought about by the use of candles, which by their very nature envelop the attention of the user into the evocative allure of the flame. Candle magick, or in this case candle imagery, involves a slightly more elaborate rite than those employing crystal energies and some preparation will be necessary. This will be the occupancy of a private darkened room, and the use of a table that may be used as a symbolic altar. The traditional usage of candle magick is, in part, allied to colour symbolism and thus when selecting a candle for use in ritual, its particular colour will correspond with the primary intention of the spell. Perhaps a combination of red (passion) and white (purity) – therefore pink – would be appropriate to candle imagery employed with the specific intention of attracting love, though you may associate your desire with an entirely different colour. A table of colour associations is given on page 145. Having prepared your ritual tools as the backdrop for the ceremony, all that remains to be done is to light the candle and to proceed to direct one's mental energies towards it. (A suitable position for the user is to be seated in a chair approximately twelve inches away from the candle at eye level with the heat haze, and with the candle perhaps in the centre of the table.) With open eyes and your line of vision slightly above the flame, reconstruct your visualised scenarios as you focus your 'objective' attention upon the heat haze. Your 'subjective' attention is upon the images in your mind's eye. This brings about a collusion between the thing seen 'objectively' (candle aura) and 'subjectively' (inner images).

Begin to create your visualised romantic episodes within the yellowy aura encircling the flame; 'see' your lover responding to you as you become immersed and at one with this 'objective' reality. When you are able to concentrate intently on this (visual distractions are at first likely to occur) then you might perform the ritual for a duration of roughly fifteen minutes. The inescapable presence of the candle flame may evoke a feeling of high drama, something mystical, profound and awe inspiring, as your projected images 'above' the flame appear to be imbued with the candle's energy as the heat rises and they are thus impressed on to the universe. To this end, consider the visualisation to be objectified, appearing as it does, 'extended' into the candle aura. The emission of heat from the flame can be considered a source of creative power in such a ceremony. However one chooses to regard the experience of candle magick, or the harmonising effects of the crystal, the efficacy of such ceremonies will depend upon your faith in the end result and your trust in the forces of attraction.

The Conclusion

The process which brings our ideals into reality, when seen in another context, consists of a meeting of internal and external worlds, almost as if the outer environment were aligning itself to what we are thinking. Scientists of the late twentieth century are asserting that consciousness plays a vital role in the creation of one's world, that the universe does not exist so much 'out there' as it does 'in here'. Paraphrasing physicist John Wheeler, the universe is brought into being by the participation of those who participate. The so-called objective world often corresponds with some dynamic activity of the psyche. Yet we did not *cause* that event to occur in the strict sense – the car breaking down unexpectedly, the good news by telephone, the house being burgled.

The omniscience of the unconscious, or the alignment of Mind and universe, when environmental phenomena correspond well with our aims and intentions, is a phenomenon that we shall perhaps never explain. It is better left that way; at least the enigma will keep physicists, philosophers and psychologists busy for some time to come. So, whilst looking forward to the future, in earnest expectation of that mysterious other person ready to enter your life, you may take heart from the fact that the 'powers that be' are silently, yet deliberately, preparing for their arrival in your world.

Table Of Symbolic Colour Associations
(For Use In Candle Magick)

Colour	Association
WHITE	Purity, illumination, 'pure spirit', inner peace, serenity, intuition.
YELLOW	Intellect, communication, learning, ability to express ideas effectively.
GOLD/ORANGE	Creativity, self-worth, inner 'riches', lust for life, integrity, sincerity of purpose.
LIGHT BLUE/PINK	Love relationships, romance, appreciation of art, social pleasures, attractiveness, feeling of harmony, sexuality (feminine).
GREEN	Material pleasures, love of nature, abundance, physicality, fertility, money and possessions.
DARK BLUE/VIOLET	Philosophical qualities, higher learning, broadening one's (mental) horizons, clarity of vision.
RED	Passion, ardour, strength, vitality, will power, initiative, sexual energies (masculine).
DARK GREEN/RUSSET	Patience, earthly wisdom, prudence, productivity, effectiveness in the concrete world.

COMMENTS ON VISUALISATION

1. Imagination is a creative force in the universe, one without which nothing can come into manifestation.

2. The universe is in essence a conglomeration of *energies*. We experience its outer forms everywhere, remaining blind to the inner essences which govern it.

3. Imagination, or the power of thought, is just such an essence, continually seeking its likeness in the world of outer manifestation.

4. Even though our normal consciousness may indicate the contrary, there is no ultimate difference between one's psyche and the events which befall one. Hence, the power inherent in the imagination may literally transform one's life.

5. The power to visualise the things we would like to see lives within us all.

6. The unconscious mind must first be reached in order to release the full potential of the power of the imagination, and relaxation is the first step along the path.

7. The ideal lifestyle of every man and woman, and the image thereof, cannot come to fruition without the guiding light of faith in its reality.

8. Always aim a little higher than the intended target. The imagination is limitless, but there is always the gravity of the physical world to consider.

9. Always conceive of a well-defined objective to which to aspire, recreating its likeness within your imagination. With repeated effort you have taken the first step towards having it.

10. We act upon our universe, and the universe consequently reacts to us. Is not the transmission of thought energy, or visualising, an action?

11. Make your intentions well known to the universe, that is, conceive of your ideal and refuse to be swayed from your path. In time you will gather the necessary forces that will turn the dream into reality.

12. The emotive power, faith, belief in your as yet unmanifested dream, must follow you wherever you may go. Don't lose it.

13. Never accept failure on your journey towards the distant goal. Beware of thoughts leading to the downward spiral where 'even that which they have shall be taken away'.

14. The need to guard carefully one's thoughts must be born in mind at all times. Whatever it is one allows in there to settle firmly shall manifest slowly but surely. Cloudy thoughts, though difficult to resist, should be cast out.

15. The unconscious mind may be likened to an infinite number of seeds about to take root; if the plants are to blossom into healthy life, they must be nurtured with the appropriate care. This means positive desire, the power of faith and a great deal of patience.

16. Perhaps one of the most effective ruses to play upon the unconscious is to behave as if you were already in possession of the desired object. This form of self-hypnosis is a powerful tool in bringing you nearer to the desired goal.

17. It is too simple to say that mental image equals manifested event – but why complicate things? Even modern science identifies energy with matter.

18. Even though it is convenient to say that the mind *causes* events to manifest, in reality there is a third factor which brings mind and event together.

19. Resist becoming over concerned with the 'when and where' of your visualised goal; the universe cannot be hurried into complying with your intentions and desires, no matter how much you may want them. But soon, you will awaken to find that your luck has changed.

20. When Nature begins to show her hand, you will know this by the coincidences that occur. These are the patterns at work which indicate that your desired goal is beginning to take form.

21. At the point when your visualised ideal finally manifests, it will appear unheralded, as if from nowhere.

AFFIRMATIONS

The mages of old would have named the following autosuggestive lines 'words of power'. As this suggests, they are affirmative statements possessing of dynamic, magical force. Of course, the 'magick' is entirely in the response called up by the emotions, which proceed to create an impression on the unconscious. Immediately following your visualisation exercise, proceed with repeating any one of the following affirmative announcements, meditating on or speaking the words slowly, and clearly. You must perform this ceremony in earnest, making the effort to believe that what you are saying is true. With sufficient repetition and sincerity, your inner mind will eventually begin to get the idea. This is a technique designed to bypass the rationalisations of the conscious, logical mind, the goal of which is to awaken the inner creative powers. To make your affirmations a success, you must begin to live the part. The affirmations are a fitting finale, rounding off the exercise and affirming (literally, making firm) the reality of your chosen goal. You may select several at once, or create your own affirmation.

Affirmations For Authority

'I have now increased and multiplied confidence in myself, and I am ready for anything!'

'I draw upon an inner core of personal self-will, energy and dynamism, to achieve my objectives – and success will be mine.'

'There is no job too large that I cannot accomplish!'

'As each new day arrives, my personal magnetism grows stronger, as my inner power increases.'

'I am entirely satisfied with myself, now that I am in a perfectly fulfilling career.'

'My sense of self-worth is blossoming to its fullest extent, as my creative talents express themselves in the universe.'

'I see myself radiating confidence, joy, health and wealth, as I put myself in touch with the creative source of all life.'

'I am a possessor of great talents, with the ability to communicate harmoniously with all types of people.'

'When dealing with others in authority, I am poised, relaxed and entirely in command of the situation.'

'I am able to create a great impression on others with my cool, self-assured personality.'

'My sense of self-worth arises from that inner part of me which is unique, alive and special.'

'Every day I grow more prosperous, from an inner core of generous, powerful, creative energy.'

'I give thanks to the universal mind for my new-found powers of self-confidence, will and determination.'

Affirmations For Friendship

This next section, as the title indicates, is dedicated to all those souls in need of a little human company, not the love and affection of a partner, but someone of the same psycho-logical stuff, with perhaps the same talents and interests. The inability to relate to others of one's own kind stems from the same inability we discovered in the previous section – that is, a general lack of confidence about oneself.

'I attract many and varied rewarding friendships, bringing warmth and pleasure into my life!'

'I constantly look for the best in people, knowing that I can bring out their most appealing qualities.'

'Having much to give in a friendship, I attract the goodwill and companionship of many different people.'

'Friends come my way easily, and I feel uplifted and happy in the presence of others.'

'I form relationships with others for I know I have much to offer in the way of warmth and company.'

'I truly appreciate the people I'm with, knowing them to be likewise healthy-minded, strong and generous.'

'I am able to bring pleasure to others, knowing myself to be an attractive creative personality.'

'As I seek to understand the true nature of those around me, I will always attract deeply fulfilling and meaningful friendships.'

'The friendship I offer has no strings attached, and thus I continually attract generous and helpful people.'

'I possess a powerful personality, and draw upon the forces of the universe to attract others.'

'Being with friends is a wonderful feeling, and I give thanks that I can share in their good company.'

'I have all the friends I need, and look forward to many more pleasurable times born of a rich and fulfilling social life.'

'I give thanks to the universal mind for the wonderful friends I meet each day.'

Affirmations For Love

And of course, we resume the ultimate and overriding theme of the book with this the last section. It introduces several salient points you might like to consider before proceeding with the rituals, and several autosuggestive lines centred around a modern 'love spell'. As the word 'love' is so ambiguous, you ought to have a reasonably clear idea of what you mean by it before bringing the appropriate imagery to bear. What *kind* of relationship are you hoping to attract? Does love – to you – mean flowers and romance, caring and sharing, pampering, sexual passion, religious ecstasy or a deep-seated emotional union? Only you will be able to answer this question. When your exercise in visualisation eventually proves to be a success, then, as the thrill of the new partner has died down a little, you ought to be able to see the partner as a reflection of some deeper, unrecognised portion of yourself. To paraphrase Crowley, you can only attract the situations in life for which you are fitted.

The following words of power are designed to stir the unconscious into bringing a partner into one's life. If you are already 'attached', they may be utilised as an additional creative force which engenders harmony and brings out the best in your relationships. You will note that most of these autosuggestive lines are phrased as a 'final state' affirmation, referring to a situation whereby the relationship is already in existence. This is quite intentional, since the unattached person using visualisation to attract a partner will fare much better if the idea can be communicated to the unconscious that the relationship is 'here and now'. Being able to see and feel oneself already in possession of the desired object is going to hasten its appearance into concrete existence. Repeat either one, or several, of the following affirmations as a conclusion to your visualising exercises (remember, slowly and earnestly) in order to enlist the aid of the inner mind.

'I open myself up to the universe and draw love and happiness into my life.'

'The creative energy flowing from me attracts healthy, happy, loving relationships into my life.'

'Being able to love someone is especially rewarding to me, and I give love knowing that it will be offered freely in return.'

'My ideal partner is here in my life at this very moment.'

'My partner and I are able to look deep within ourselves and discover an abundant source of loving energy.'

'Each time I look into my partner's face, I know that love is there for me.'

'My life is whole, meaningful, complete, and filled with the happiness that comes from a loving relationship.'

'I am filled with a warm and beautiful feeling when I am with my partner, knowing them from the heart.'

'I have much to give in a relationship, and the more love I give, the more I receive.'

'When I think of the many more wonderful times we will share together, I know that my search to find the right person has all been worth it.'

'As I open myself up to positive emotions, I know that my relationship will prove to be successful and enriching.'

'I give thanks to the universal mind for paving the way to a wonderful, loving relationship.'

WHAT THEY SAID ABOUT LIFE, LOVE AND THE SEXES

'At any given moment, life is completely senseless. But viewed over a period it seems to reveal itself as an organism existing in time, having a purpose, tending in a certain direction.' Aldous Huxley.

'A single event can awaken within us a stranger totally unknown to us. To live is to be slowly born.' Antoine de Saint Exupery

'The man who has no inner life is the slave of his surroundings.' Henri Frederic Amiel

'You've got to keep fighting – you've got to risk your life every six months to stay alive.' Elia Kazan

'He who desires but acts not breeds pestilence.' William Blake

'The supreme happiness of life is the conviction that we are loved.' Victor Hugo

'It would seem that love never seeks real perfection, and even fears it. It delights only in the perfection it has itself imagined: it is like those kings who recognise no greatness except their own works.' Roland Barthes

'It would be impossible to "love" anyone or anything one knew completely. Love is directed to what lies hidden in its object.' The Zohar

'He who lives without jealousy does not truly love.' The Zohar

'Selfishness is one of the qualities to inspire love.' Nathaniel Hawthorne

'Love, like fire, cannot survive without continual movement, and it ceases to live as soon as it ceases to hope or fear.' La Rochefoucauld

'Christianity has done a great deal for love by making a sin of it.' Anatole France

'The loving are the daring.' Bayard Taylor

'Little privations are easily endured when the heart is better treated than the body.' Jean Jacques Rousseau

'The magic of first love is our ignorance that it can ever end.' Benjamin Disraeli

'Love cannot accept what it is. Everywhere on earth it cries out against kindness, compassion, intelligence, everything that leads to compromise. Love demands the impossible, the absolute, the sky on fire, inexhaustible springtime, life after death, and death itself transfigured into eternal life.' Camus

'True love is like seeing ghosts; we all talk about it but few of us have ever seen one.' La Rochefoucauld.

'It is absurd to say that a man can't love one woman all the time as it is to say that a violinist needs several violins to play the same piece of music.' Honore de Balzac

'Men who do not make advances to women are apt to become victims to women who make advances to them.' Bagehot

'I like men to behave like men. I like them strong and childish.' Francoise Sagan

'Women deprived of the company of men pine, men deprived of the company of women become stupid.' Anton Chekhov

'It is a mistake to speak of a bad choice in love, since, as soon as a choice exists it can only be bad.' Marcel Proust

' It takes all sorts to make a sex.' Saki

'What is most beautiful in virile men is something femi-nine. What is most beautiful in feminine women is some-thing masculine.' Susan Sontag

SELECTED BIBLIOGRAPHY

Arroyo, Stephen, *Astrology, Psychology and the Four Elements*, CRCS, 1975.

Bishop, Beta/Mcneil, Pat, *Below the Belt*, Coventure, 1977.

Boase, Roger, *The Origin and Meaning of Courtly Love*, Manchester University Press, 1977.

Bonewitz, Ra, *Cosmic Crystals*, Aquarian Press, 1983.

Brontë, Emily, *Wuthering Heights*, Penguin Classics, 1988.

Buckland, Raymond, *The Tree – The Complete Book of Saxon Witchcraft*, Samuel Weiser, 1974.

Cowan, Connell/Kinder, Melvyn, *Smart Women, Foolish Choices*, Bantam Books, 1985.

Conway, David, *Magic: An Occult Primer*, Jonathan Cape, 1972.

Conway, David, *Secret Wisdom: The Occult Universe Explored*, Aquarian Press, 1987.

Farrar, Janet and Stewart, *The Witches Goddess*, Robert Hale, 1987.

Fowles, John, *The French Lieutenant's Woman*, Pan Books, 1987.

Fryer, Peter, *Mrs Grundy: Studies in English Prudery*, Dobson Books, 1963.

Gawain, Shakti, *Creative Visualisation*, Bantam Books, 1982.

Gawain, Shakti, *Living In The Light*, Eden Grove Editions, 1988.

Gullo, Stephen/Church, Connie, *Loveshock*, Simon and Schuster, 1988.

Goldberg, Herb, *The New Male-Female Relationship*, Coventure, 1984.

Greene, Liz, *Relating*, Aquarian Press.

Greene, Liz, *Astrology For Lovers*, Unwin Paperbacks, 1986.

Harding, M. Esther, *The Way of All Women*, Rider & Co. 1971.

Harding, M. Esther, *The I and The Not I*, Princeton University Press, 1965.

Harding, M. Esther, *Woman's Mysteries*, Century Hutchinson, 1989.

Hugo, Howard E. (Ed.), *The Romantic Reader*, Viking Press Inc., 1960.

Koran, Al, *Bring Out The Magic In Your Mind*, A. Thomas, 1964.

Lao Tzu, *Tao Te Ching*, Penguin, 1963.

Lawrence, D.H., *The Complete Short Novels*, Penguin English Library, 1982.

Peck, M. Scott, *The Road Less Travelled*, Rider & Co., 1985.

Samuels, M & N., *Seeing With The Mind's Eye*, Random House, 1976.

Simmons, Charles, *Your Subconscious Power*, Wilshire Book Co., 1965.

Sternberg, R.J./Barnes, M.L. (Ed's.), *The Psychology of Love*, Yale University Press, 1985.

Stewart, R.J., *The Prophetic Vision of Merlin*, Arkana, 1986.

Tolstoy, Nikolai, *The Quest for Merlin*, Hamish Hamilton, 1985.

Watts, Alan W., *Nature, Man and Woman*, Vintage Books, 1970.

Wickes, Frances G., *The Inner World of Choice*, Coventure, 1977.

Wilson, Annie, *The Wise Virgin: The Missing Link Between Man and Woman*, Turnstone Press, 1979.

INDEX

Affirmations, 148
  for authority, 148–9
  for friendship, 149–50
  for love, 151–7
Age of Reason, 17
Air, 63–6
Anima, 72–6, 81, 82, 90, 105, 123, 124, 138
Animus, 73–4, 75, 79, 81, 82, 91–103, 105, 123, 124
Aquarian Age, 7, 21, 107–8, 110
Archetypes, 29, 31, 33, 73, 82, 84, 99, 105, 123, 137
Artemis-Diana, 134
Astrology, 10, 45–68, 106
Attraction, Laws of, 8
Awareness, 13

Baudelaire, Charles, 16
Blake, William, 19
Bonewitz, Ra, 140, 141
Brain hemispheres, 49
Brontë, Emily, 16, 17, 67, 78
Buddhism, Zen, 36, 138
Byron, 16, 17

Camus, Albert, 19
Candle visions, 142–3
Cervantes, Miguel, 15
Colour symbolism, 142, 145
Cosmic Crystals, 140
Crystal visions, 140–2

Devil, the, 105, 106
Divination, 7
Dream lover, 8

Earth, 57–63
Ecstasy, 15
Elements, the four, 46–50
Enigma, 14
Eros, 12

Faith, 125, 126
Fate, 69, 74
Father complex, 14
Faulkner, William, 85
Femininity, 23, 29–34
Feminism, 22, 25–7, 33
Fire, 50–7
Fowles, John, 87
French Lieutenant's Woman, 87–91
Freud, Sigmund, 13

Goethe, 18, 19
Grail Quest, 112

Hades-Pluto, 101, 133
Heisenberg, Werner, 45–6
Hekate, 133–44
Hero's quest, 28
Hubris, 86

Image-making, 123
Imagery, mental, 8
Instincts, 21

Jung, C.G., 10, 30, 72, 74

Lawrence, D.H., 99, 101
Logos, 91–103
Love,
    courtly, 17–18
    definition of, 8
    objects, 85–103
    poppet, 134–5
    potion, 119
    quotations, 153–4
    rules of, 18

Magick, 105, 109, 119
Mandrake, 135
Masculinity, 23, 29–34
Melville, 16
Mental energy, 120
Merlin, 39, 104, 109–13, 120, 134
Middle Ages, 105, 135–7
Mind, 120, 126, 129–30, 144
Morals, 20
'Mother Bunch's Closet', 136–7
Mother complex, 4

New Testament, 106

Occult, 7, 40
Opposites, attraction of, 29–34

Paraphiliac, 20
Partnerships, 13
Payne, Cynthia, 24
Persephone, 101
Projection, 87, 90, 123
Psychology, Depth, 19
Pygmalion, 85, 104–5
Reik, Theodore, 13
Relationships, personal, 10

Ritual, 119, 120, 122, 125, 126,
    140–3
    Tantric, 38
Romance, 12
Romantics, 10, 16–19
Rousseau, 16
Russell, Bertrand, 15

Security, 123
Sex,
    aim-inhibited, 13
    magick, 25, 34
    opposite, 13
Sexism, 22
Shaman, 110
Shelley, 16, 19
Soul, 14
    mate, 77–84

Table Round, the, 111–12
Tantra, 38–41
Tao, 10, 35–8, 39, 73
    of Love, 41–4
Tao Te Ching, 36, 37
Tarot, 113–18
Thought Forces, 121
Troubadours, 17–18

Unconscious, the, 14, 21, 30, 32,
    71, 75, 82–3, 126, 127, 134, 144

Virgin And The Gypsy, 99–102
Visualisation, 12, 104, 199–32,
    138–44
    definition of, 120

Water, 67–8
Wuthering Heights, 17, 67, 78–81

Yield To The Night, 102–3
Yin-Yang, 30, 36, 38, 46, 73, 134